The
Panic Years

The
Panic Years

DOREE LEWAK

A Guide to Surviving Smug Married Friends,
Bad Taffeta, and Life on
the Wrong Side of 25 Without a Ring

BROADWAY BOOKS

New York

BROADWAY

PUBLISHED BY BROADWAY BOOKS

Copyright © 2008 by Doree Lewak

All Rights Reserved

Published in the United States by Broadway Books, an imprint of
The Doubleday Broadway Publishing Group, a division of Random
House, Inc., New York. www.broadwaybooks.com

BROADWAY BOOKS and its logo, a letter B bisected on the
diagonal, are trademarks of Random House, Inc.

Library of Congress Cataloging-in-Publication Data
Lewak, Doree.
  The Panic years : a guide to surviving smug married friends, bad
taffeta, and life on the wrong side of 25 without a ring / Doree
Lewak.—1st ed.
    p. cm.
    1. Single women—Psychology.   2. Single women—Social
conditions.   3. Single women—Conduct of life.   I. Title.
  HQ800.2.L47 2008
  306.81'53—dc22   2007036225

ISBN 978-0-7679-2599-0

PRINTED IN THE UNITED STATES OF AMERICA

10 9 8 7 6 5 4 3 2 1

First Edition

Contents

Part

TWO: You Have Him Right Where You Want Him:
*Stay on Course and You Can Start Booking Caterers
by the End of the Year*

Part
Three: The Silver Lining in Being Single

The Panic Years Key:

PF (Potential Fiancé)

SPS (Self-Pitying Spinster)

WMD (Witless Married Dullard)

NBNMM (Nice, But Not Marriage Material)

S-I-Ts (Sluts-in-Training)

SAD (Singles Against Doubles)

SAP (Settled and Pious)

USAPR (Underemployed Singles Against Paying Retail)

Confessions of a Panicker

Anointing myself the Panic Years Pioneer brings with it great responsibility. To panic in solitude is a lonely cause. But in truth, I panic not in solitude but in solidarity! I walk among you every day without you even knowing it. I sit next to you—eyes averted—on the subway, and stand next to you clawing through the Bloomingdales sales racks. I look like you and I talk like you. You'd never know there was a Potential Fiancé (PF) predator among you, but if you look closely, you'll see a stunning little blonde looking into the middle distance, looking for her PF. My cool girl-about-town exterior belies my true inner panic, churning furiously, restlessly, internally.

Something has dealt a mighty blow to my happiness—and that something is other people's happiness. The detestable kind of happiness that only newly minted married friends can spew. You know the type—those friends who are married for five minutes and will exult during the salad course, "You have to try this! Marriage is the best feeling in the world!" in perpetual self-celebration. A Self-Pitying Spinster's sanity is but a flickering ember, and the mountain of wedding invitations from her "best friends" is the mighty wind that threatens to blow it out. And so this is where my Panic Memoir—or Panoir—begins.

My name is Doree Samantha Lewak and I'm a reformed panicker of the highest order. My journey through the highs and lows of the Panic Years has been a rocky one—inadvertently taking down a few PF pawns along the way—but I can proudly declare myself panic-free, and with this book I want to help you get there too.

Allow me to fill in some of the gaps in my panic saga. I'm single and I just turned twenty-seven, which is really just a nice way of saying thirty. Damn euphemisms—let's call a spade a spade, or in this case, a spinster a spinster. I know what I am (just the teensiest bit self-obsessed, but with high cheekbones and even higher hopes to nail down that investment banker) and I know what I'm not (married, or at least sporting a garish, if not killer, 2.1-carat round solitaire that's as blinding as it is show-stopping).

I know that I had a boyfriend, who, coincidentally or not, recently booked a one-way ticket to the Middle East and is trying—unsuccessfully, though I must applaud his efforts—to convince me that I'd never be able to handle the unforgiving heat. The poor guy actually thinks the 112-degree days in the shade will dilute my determination to get a proposal out of him. I haven't doggedly practiced saying, "Honey, you know this dry heat really isn't that bad!" for two months only to quit five minutes before the matrimonial miracle.

I know that in certain dim light and standing next to a haggard thirty-three-year-old, I can easily pass for twenty-two. I know that perfunctorily going on a blind date with Eccentric Eye Patch Guy—no pun intended—is not helping me keep the panic at bay. And I know—the way you just know when a force greater than you has penetrated the depths of your soul—that the Panic Years have gripped me.

It was late 2002, when I was but a twenty-two-year-old effervescent innocent ready to make her mark, that the term "Panic Years" first entered my vernacular. It was a Saturday night and I'd piggybacked onto my sister and her married friends, who had dinner plans (never a good sign). But I was only twenty-two, after all, and not remotely concerned with my romantic status: what was the rush to date, let alone date seriously? I still got away with posing as a high school student to get a discount on haircuts, why would I hurry to settle down when I had the world on a golden string? So when the Settled and Pious (SAP) Mark asked if I was dating anyone, I quickly shrugged him off and joked, "Well, you're off the market, so what else is there to look forward to out there in the dating pool?" But Mark didn't give me the reaction I was hoping for. He didn't laugh and he didn't play along. What he did do, however, was instill in me a state of fear so palpable, so deeply embedded, that his corrosiveness has consumed me ever since. "Oh, that's okay," he said smugly. "You still have a few years before you really start to panic."

"Panic? There are Panic Years?" I gulped, my eyes expanding wider than the saucers of milk I'd soon be leaving for my single-gal litter of cats at home. "Is it contagious?" I demanded, with increasing alarm. Mark just gave me a knowing smirk—knowing full well that his verbal bullet had torn right through my heart—and moved on to another topic, leaving me speechless, confused, and very, very afraid. And this is where the seeds of incipient panic about my single status were sown, and when getting 15 percent off on a haircut suddenly didn't seem so exhilarating anymore.

Since then, life had generally been the stuff of muted discontent eventually giving way to singles' ennui.

High Priestess of Panic

Sure enough, it all fell into place the morning of my twenty-sixth birthday, just as legend (and Mark) said it would. I awoke from my otherwise peaceful repose in the seaside Mediterranean villa where I was vacationing—and where sun-kissed Stavroses and Nikoses abounded—with an unmistakable case of the single-at-twenty-six-and-starting-to-feel-like-I-can't-breathe thing wresting control of my system. Was this sinking feeling a foreboding omen for a marriage-less year to come? What other conclusions could I draw? It was panic season—the predetermined writing was on the white stuccoed wall!

The catalyst was clear: the night before, my boyfriend at the time had sent me a birthday e-mail with a cryptic line that haunted me: "I wish you everything you wish for yourself on your birthday, plus something else." What did "something else" mean? An engagement ring? For me to be stricken with a bolt of lightning? (Were the chances I'd get either about the same?) Something about his stunningly glib and evasive remark woke me up to the reality that this relationship probably didn't have a viable future and that, at twenty-six, I didn't want to invest in a person who didn't want to make a long-term investment in me. The breakup took place a few weeks after my return, when my hope for our future, and coincidentally my tan, had all but faded irrevocably.

That fateful birthday marked the unequivocal crossover into my Panic Years abyss—the murky, yet all too clear reality that those "expression lines" on my face aren't going to reverse themselves and that the "You'll get there!" affirmations from my enthused engaged and married friends were creeping into conversations with a little too much frequency and self-satisfaction for my taste.

Applying eye cream at night had become futile. The deluge of tears in bed about it not happening for me routinely diluted my eighty-five-dollar-an-ounce cream always ending in "de la mer" that I don't think softened any lines anyway. My best friend's wedding at the time didn't help matters. Serving as her maid of honor, I carried off a puffy, burgundy taffeta number—which can only be described as a really shiny rhinestone-encrusted sleeping bag—with the refinement I always knew would surface one day when I needed it badly enough.

The day of the wedding, the rabbi—who I'd known since grade school—was all too happy to nod to the bride and make the pronouncement that I'd be next. Smiling through clenched teeth, I tried to rationalize that he meant no harm by his soothsaying, but I just couldn't let it go and sheepishly had to ask him to knock on wood. Despite the beard masking most of his face, I could discern an unmistakable expression of bewilderment and disgust when he explained, "The Jews don't believe in superstitions. Knocking on wood is pagan and I can't do it." I was ultimately forced to listen to a well-intentioned, although unnecessary, speech about how real Jews don't fall prey to superstitions if they truly believe in G-d. If he had only knocked on wood three times like I asked him, we wouldn't have wasted precious cocktail-hour time and I wouldn't be plagued by his hex to this day.

But for me, the Panic Years have been about more than

bullying my childhood rabbi into suspending his beliefs. They've inspired me to do much crazier things, all in the name of securing a proposal. They are what led me to book a B&B in the Berkshires for me and a new PF four months in advance because a fall proposal—overlapping with the fantastic jazz festival at Tanglewood—is what I'd had my heart set on for years. What's more ideal than a lakeside engagement against that fall foliage backdrop? Probably having a willing boyfriend and, upon some honest introspection, sanity.

Or take, for example, the Rosh Hashanah card I sent to my now ex-PF's parents in Connecticut. Getting caught up in the spirit of the Jewish New Year, and the deep philosophical meaning behind it, and after writing all my well wishes, I ended with a "See you at the wedding!" sign-off.

Normal people with filters just don't do that.

So, yes, at twenty-six, the Panic had driven me to make just as big a fool of myself as I did when I was six, when I engineered a bicycle accident with my closest playground pal, whose attention I desperately coveted. He saw right through the thin plotting—there's not much injury you can suffer with training wheels, after all—and fled the scene of the accident. I may have hit the cement hard, but the plan to cement our love never quite took off. So now I try my best to counsel my cousin, Ava, who, even at her tender young age, just got a mighty dose of the agony and the ecstasy of love. She recently proposed marriage to her first-grade classmate Tyler, rocking classroom water coolers all over school. Tyler called her crazy, declared, "You're stupid!" and hasn't spoken to her since.

Typical guy.

I saw a distraught and dejected Ava blubbering about romantic doom and reassured her that Tyler just had the classic knee-jerk guy reaction (he's so textbook, even for a six-year-

old). Confused, he couldn't handle his feelings or the situation. Quite the tableau for me, but better that Ava learn the
pains of love now than repeat that mistake in twenty years. In
fact, Ava isn't too young to start taking precautions to stave off
the Panic Years by the time she reaches syndrome peak. My
favorite mantra is, of course, *it's never too early to panic!*

For a while, the Panic was a plague with no foreseeable
cure; it was an incarceration that extended to every mental
and emotional realm. I was handed that bitter reminder with
a little too much regularity—especially when the gaggle of
single girls gathered around for the bouquet toss at friends'
weddings whittled down little by little; with time, it was just
me, the seven-year-old flower girl with a dress even puffier
and more unflattering than mine, and the closeted lesbian
cousin (as if that navy pantsuit and combat boots combo for a
June wedding wasn't skywriting her sexuality for the masses).
During the holidays, going home to my old room was one
big 'ole psychotherapy bill in the making. My sister's boxed
wedding gown with the see-through plastic staring sympa-
thetically at me from the corner is not the stuff of which
panic-free lullabies are made. And my dad piping in, "You
know there's a statute of limitations on that dress!" didn't necessarily help either.

There is a Jewish theory rooted in Talmudic trunks of
thought that a woman's soul mate is identified forty days before birth—a belief that has always seemed to bring a certain
level of solace to panic practitioners of all faiths. Go out there
and live your life, the belief says, and you'll eventually be
aligned with your soul mate; what's meant to be will be. This
charming idea might keep our fears at bay for a while, but
when a woman gets to a certain unspeakable age—I'm thinking twenty-six or so—these theories are no match for the in-
herent Panic. At a relationship class I once attended, "How to

Land Your Soul Mate or the Closest Thing to Him Before Your Next Dental Cleaning," two self-pitying spinsters (SPSs) meditated over another convenient theory—the "seven soul mates" theory, positing that there are seven existing soul mates for every one person. Forget seven soul mates—I'm not even asking for one soul mate! How about one guy without a unibrow who knows how to reformat my hard drive?

So What Exactly Are "The Panic Years" and Are They Contagious?

"The Panic Years" represent a sociological phenomenon that single women confront in their twenties—or when symptoms of TMJ first kick in due to fake-smiling your way through the last seven of your friends' engagements. In some extreme cases I've heard of In Utero Panic—panic of the prenatal set—but again, these are all unconfirmed reports, and subject to a mother's personal interpretation of what extreme kicking and wailing actually mean. The Panic Years describe the marked change in a woman's dating agenda, when she stops dating for a fling and starts dating for a ring. It's the reason why, after the age of twenty-five, every guy is wary of you and your mom's neon-loud nails sinking into his singledom. No longer are you primarily interested in the transient and unfulfilling ways of hooking up; now you're interested in tracking down your loser college boyfriend with whom you wasted three years— the best years!—of your life and blinding him with your 1.9-carat princess-cut solitaire and flashing him a copy of your wedding contract with the Waldorf Astoria.

It's that undeniable feeling of panic that cuts through

layer after layer, choking you at your core, underscoring the immediacy of the problem that's suddenly causing the room to inexplicably close in on you. You find yourself sitting at home alone on a Sunday morning, wondering if you'll be alone forever. The first time you catch yourself slip aloud—"I don't care about finding a meaningful relationship, I just want to be married!"—is another useful panic barometer.

Yes, even for the self-assured, career-minded girls of today, the Panic Years are an undeniable cultural condition gripping the twenties-plus singles set in America. Even if you've never succumbed to middle-of-the-night cold sweats about being single, you've probably entertained a passing thought about why the ugliest girl in your sorority got engaged before you. The intensified pressure to get married is all too real, especially when those in your inner circle start leaving the singles' fold, and the over-the-top, in-your-face wedding industry that's taken on a life of its own in recent years is an unrelenting jack-hammer chipping away at your singles psyche. The very fact that terms like "bridezilla," the designer Vera Wang, and names of celebrity wedding planners are part of our vernacular all add up to mounting Panic. It's these and countless other factors that have led to this epidemic sweeping the country—and filling even the sanest single girl with self-doubt.

As long as there are thirty-six-year-old men like Daniel from D.C. who can still pass for twenty-seven and can still "get away with dating twenty-five-year-olds" without a glimmer of desire to settle down until the last bottle of Propecia is recalled, the Panic Years will only intensify. It's not an ephemeral trend, but an entrenched part of our dating landscape. And if you ever want to graduate beyond career panicker status, I suggest you start your marriage campaign now. Or get very comfortable with "alone time."

Remember: Forty may be the new thirty, but according

to the media, our parents, and the wedding industrial complex, waking up on the wrong side of twenty-five without a ring is still the new panic.

THE GENESIS OF THE PANIC YEARS: WHO'S TO BLAME FOR THIS MESS?

The man responsible for launching a thousand panickers? Pope Innocent III, that myopic Catholic leader who, in one swift papal motion, created an eternal ripple effect of biblical proportions. He's the one we can thank for the concept of an "engagement period," dragging out the envy and drawing the ire of singles everywhere by sparking the tradition of an engagement ring. Singles' last enjoyable supper was savored in 1215 CE—a grim year for singles everywhere—with the inception of said engagement period. Pope Innocent III—not so innocent, it turns out. At least he achieved what he set out to do: make believers out of all of us. There's not one panicker left who doesn't believe we'd be better off today if he just kept his holy mouth shut!

A United Nations—of Panickers, That Is . . .

Want to know why Entenmann's stock has recently spiked? The latest Census Bureau study revealed the median age of a U.S. bride is 25.1 years old—and in outliers like Utah it's a tender 21.9 years old. So basically, if you're a tenth-grader out in Provost and you're not engaged, you're totally screwed! Really, these days anyone of voting age (we're talking *American Idol* voting here) is more or less considered a "mature bride." So while eager teenage girls are applying for a driver's license, why not kill two birds with one stone and apply for a marriage license too? Thank goodness for holdouts in D.C., where the median age for a Beltway Bride is thirty. Can someone pass the stale glazed mini-doughnuts, please?

While these bridal buzz kill statistics would suggest that every American woman too young to remember Pluto as a planet is already married, a 2007 study sent women's hearts—and hopes—soaring. It revealed that 51 percent of women are living single in America; so just like Republicans in Congress, married women no longer control the House! Now under normal circumstances, we would flash this figure as our get-out-of-panicking-free card, but in fact the cultural reverberations reflect the opposite effect. Instead of letting half the American female population collectively legitimize our single status sans shame—and for that matter, take the sting out of being single—the Panic has never felt more pervasive, giving rise to the greater Panic Years phenomenon.

So the real question becomes, If it's now culturally acceptable to be single—and society is seemingly giving single women a thumbs-up about our "lifestyle choice"—then why are so many of us still panicking? In an age when women are hungrier for more, in terms of our careers and our personal goals, we are just as hungry for a ring and marriage as ever before—despite the message 51 percent of us are sending. Just because we've crossed a new cultural milestone doesn't necessarily mean we're toasting it. (And we're especially not toasting it at other people's weddings!)

Are these statistics a true testament to a lifestyle choice we've come to embrace in the new cultural dating climate? While they seem to be signaling freedom and a new era for American women, we somehow feel even more ashamed that deep down we still want to get married. Only unlike women of previous generations, we're forced to hide our shame and disappointment under a shining coat of autonomy. We shroud ourselves in shame because we're not married, and then chastise ourselves for even caring in the first place. In this ever-confusing era for women, even the strongest and most successful of us are reduced to panicking in silence. After all the cultural and political hurdles we've cleared, we're still a group that panics into our pillows at night—to hell with that exorbitantly expensive eye cream!

I've come to the realization that even in a postfeminist frontier where women are no longer secretaries, but secretaries of state, every woman—no matter how successful, attractive, and confident—will at one point or another fall prey to the fangs of the Panic phenomenon, even if we bristle at the very thought *right now*.

No matter how common singles are in our society, singleness is still considered a failure—a by-product of the mixed message driven home for decades that while we're supposedly a self-sufficient sex, we are nonetheless considered a failure if we don't have a marital future.

Panickers Without Borders

With all the talk of homegrown, domestic panicking, let's explore to what degree the seeds of panic are spreading around the globe. Does the notion of a panic pandemic—or panpanic, if you will—really exist outside of our culture of nuptial pressure or is it just our society that foments this panic propaganda? Can a panicker's wails of nonmarital woe on one continent echo throughout the rest of the panicked world? Have the Panic Years replaced McDonald's golden arches as the new universal phenomenon? Let's explore fellow panickers' plights around the globe.

Perhaps the rest of the free world can take a lesson from Mao's playbook. These days, instead of acquitting themselves as delicate flowers in order to land a husband, China's female population now flaunt their brainpower, not helplessness. Although still completely under the choke hold of Communism in every sense of the word, at least women can panic of their own accord, not because the government says so. Now that's progress. And while they don't normally date before the age of twenty, most Chinese women marry the first man they date anyway, so there's not really time to panic. Sure, most couples are ill suited and unhappy, but so the hell what? At least they're married! As the matchmaker in *Fiddler on the Roof* always cheerfully says, "Even the worst husband is better than no husband!" Now that's an international Panic flag that any culture could proudly wave!

But I'd like to offer a hearty salute to Sweden, where marriage is strictly optional. If you were like most of Sweden's female community—blond-haired, buxom, and quite the slalom skier—you wouldn't be so eager to settle down either, even in the off-season. Moreover, a good number of Swedes have kids *before* marriage and tie the knot only after many years together. In such a progressive society, the Panic isn't even on their radar.

Similarly, finding a way to say "Panic Years" in Portuguese is an exercise about as futile as looking for a homely girl on the beaches of Rio; all those well-tanned and -toned Glamazons have handily resisted the Panic. It takes a lot more than being unmarried at thirty-one to crack these Brazilian nuts. Sure, they only have one thing on their minds, but at least it isn't Panic.

So while the Panic Years is a universal concept that SPSs of any stripe can appreciate, it's a condition much less pervasive in foreign cultures. Why is Panic considerably less pronounced worldwide than in the United States? My own feeling is that it's a reflection of our achievement-oriented culture, where expectations to excel—in every area of life—are heightened. We want to hit all the right benchmarks at the appropriate times. But even in a world in which women are experiencing unparalleled—and unprecedented—freedoms and opportunity, somehow, on some level, the Panic still pervades. We can break all the glass ceilings we want, but we still can't shatter the social stigma of being single.

GEOPOLITICAL PANIC SEEN 'ROUND THE WORLD

	Age	Middle East	West
Men	24	Goatherding and loving it	Beer guzzling through a straw between breasts of a random Cancún barmaid and loving it
Women	24	Popping out babies	Popping diet pills
Men	30	Producing crude oil in the desert	Producing crude jokes in desperation
Women	30	Wearing a veil of modesty	Wearing a veil of personal shame

The average age of a Middle Eastern groom is a respectable twenty-seven, the average age for a bride: a ripe old twenty-two. Sure, fifteen-year-old girls in the Middle East are often sold into marriage by parents drowning in debt, but surely a similar mind-set can translate to the New World. In especially lean times, you may want to start thinking about lobbying for legislation to reinstate arranged marriage by dowry. Just be sure your dad can scrounge up a couple of mules from his connected accountant friends.

The Panicked Pilgrim: How Far Will You Go to Outrun the Panic?

If you are to give yourself a competitive advantage geographically, move where the numbers work in your favor! Have you given serious consideration yet to Alaska? Alaskan men outnumber women ten to one, a fun factoid that should brighten those dark skies you'll experience twenty hours a day.

On the flipside, people have always ballyhooed New York's bloated population of Starbucks and single women, but this isn't merely a campaign SPSs have launched to dissuade fellow panickers from moving to Manhattan. Single women in the Big Apple outnumber their male counterparts by 200,000! So if you're looking to move to where the men are, don't opt for a suicide mission in Manhattan or a similar location with a notoriously lopsided male–female split.

Recognizing the Panic

Few women want to admit that they're panicked; even fewer recognize the symptoms. Often it's something that we battle internally but are loath to outwardly express—even to our closest confidantes. If you feel like you might be on the fringes, there are some telltale signs to look for. For instance, you *want* to be happy for your *younger* sister, who just became engaged, but suddenly your heart is clogged with deep contempt for this onetime gawky hanger-on you'd affectionately nicknamed PigBaby.

Besides generalized feelings of desperation and loneliness, and a body sagging in areas that used to be considered your calling card, there are certain scenarios that can accelerate the onset of the panic. Even if you're someone who has never hatched a diabolical scheme to sabotage your friend's wedding, or thought the Panic could penetrate your durable wall of sanity, watch out for these subtle but insidious scenarios that start creeping into everyday life:

SCENARIO #1: Your twenty-three-year-old jejune but dear friend just announced her engagement . . . to the guy she's been dating for two months. You can't even get the guy you've been seeing for two months to take you out on a Saturday night! Welcome to the Panic Years!

SCENARIO #2: You're a bridesmaid at four of your best friends' weddings and you're fake-smiling while posing in a sickening taffeta number knowing you're stuck at the singles table. The Panic Years have arrived.

SCENARIO #3: Your mom's well-meaning but agonizingly suffocating best friend, Linda, has a "nice guy for you," peppered by an extra "You're not getting any younger." Great, so you're not married and at the behest of your mother, you start using anti-aging cream too. This has Panic Years written all over it.

SCENARIO #4: After three months of dating someone, it's not working out and you decide to end it, only to hear that he never thought you were going out in the first place and won't accept calling it a breakup. So you've been going out with someone who never thought you were "really dating" in the first place— this can induce the Panic Years more effectively than anything else.

SCENARIO #5: Instead of clothes, a handbag, or even a nice dinner, your smugly saddled friends chip in for an eHarmony subscription for your twenty-eighth-birthday gift—without irony. P-P-Panic Years!

YOUR PERSONAL PANIC TIMELINE:

You at age 22:   Aww, look how cute Beth and Brian are!

You at age 23:   Wow, I wish I could find a nice guy like Brian.

You at age 24:   Hmm, Brian's brother Josh and his fi-ancée don't look as happy as they used to. Maybe I'll ask Brian if Josh might want to meet up sometime.

You at age 24½: Doesn't Brian know anyone for me!? I mean, he has plenty of single friends and I cannot understand why he wouldn't want to set me up! It's not like I smack of desperation, do I?!

You at age 25:   Why isn't Josh returning any of my calls?!!! Even at his wedding, I could tell he was eyeing me and when I inter-cepted the bouquet, I swear I caught him winking at me!

How to Use this Book

The book is ostensibly a marriage manual. Under the sur-face, though, lies a tome brimming with tools designed to combat the very panic that drives women like you and me to mental and emotional incarceration, hindering your chances of finding a partner. The panic is self-defeating, and one of my goals is to puncture the layers of false information we've been fed all these years and help you figure out what's important to you on your own instead of simply accepting things because they've been woven into the fabric of our culture for so long.

The advice disseminated in this book extends from dating tips—how to date with dignity and when to acknowledge that you're not just digging deep, but mining through dating wastelands in your search for a proposal—to relationship road maps to the altar to finally moving beyond the Panic for good. If you're like Monica, twenty-six, from New York City, whose roommate barged into her room at 3 a.m., complaining that her sleep was unceremoniously disturbed by what she called Monica's "negative energy" seeping through the cheap plaster wall one night when Monica was wallowing in the Panic, then this book will be your indispensable coping tool.

Or if you're like Samantha, pushing thirty—like twenty-seven is even considered part of your twenties anymore—who acknowledges, "I'm literally going to die if one more of my friends gets married now; I seriously think I'll have a nervous breakdown," then you've come to the right book.

You, like so many of us, suffer from a syndrome that is now being legitimized. It has a name and, more important, a solution. Rest assured that you are not alone with your panic, not without help, and certainly not without a no-fail plan to get you through it. Believe me, matrimonial mishaps seemed to find me like L.A.'s Scientology Celebrity Centre finds pod people, but I and the dozens of other women whose stories appear in the pages that follow are passing our own essential coping tools on to you.

The Panic Years is for those who feel that swelling panic and have no outlet or release for it. It's for those orphaned by parents now shifting their focus to younger sisters' weddings instead of your recent work promotion. I remember that deep feeling of despair, but I've also learned how to rise above it, how to conquer it, and how to outsmart it! I hope you will find hope and humor in these pages and that the book will restore your faith and confidence, both in finding someone and in yourself.

Like the millions of women in my quandary, when confronted with the panic, I'd obsess, I'd self-destruct, and then I'd obsess some more. For this reason, I believe that advice and help can be dispensed only from one former Self-Pitying Spinster (SPS) to another for the message to really ring true. And there's nothing I'd rather do than make sure the message is heard loud and clear. In this book, I help you identify your degree of panic, understand the conditions that induce the Panic, and determine what course of action you need to take in order to feel content in your single life now, while also getting on your married way. *The Panic Years* will show you how to play the game and bring back a husband, and no one— besides the slower-moving, less motivated SPSs you had to trample along the way—will get hurt. After all, you haven't slept with Tiffany's diamond buying guide under your pillow for the past three years just so you can identify an SI1, E grade diamond on command for your health!

So put down that magazine article titled "How to Make Your Wrists Look 10 Pounds Thinner NOW!" and start reading the ever more relevant "How to Make Your Ring Finger Look Sleeker Than Ever!" article for your soon-to-be spoken-for ring finger! Say good-bye to the Panic Years blues and stop playing that sorry-sounding harmonica. Let's get started!

WARNING!
THERE'S NO SUCH THING AS A SOUL MATE

This book entertains no illusions of cosmic connections, mental synergy, or—shut this book right now and toss your empty dance card if you buy into this—soul mates. The term is such a false construct that it doesn't even pass my Microsoft Word spell check, further attesting to its illegitimacy! If Microsoft doesn't recognize soul mates, then by extension neither does Bill Gates—and he's rich! Anyone with that much money can't be wrong. So with that logic, the evidence is perfectly clear: Bill Gates and I refute the notion of "soul mate." What more proof do you need, ladies?

While exaggerating slightly, I see all too often how many people get hung up on the elusive, if not intangible, concept of a perfect match; and despite deep stabs of panic, they pass over real prospects in the interest of finding this Bill Gates–condemned illusion. It's time to stop chasing the dream of a soul mate and start dating for actual results.

Quiz: How Panicked Are You?

Identifying your level of panic is essential to moving beyond it with humor and dignity on your way to finding your own Potential Fiancé (PF). When you determine how far along you are on the slippery slope we call the Panic Years, then you can learn the best strategies for overcoming them, even if you are loath to lump yourself in with this group of loud and proud panickers. Sometimes the warning signs are easy to miss—so take the quiz and find out for yourself! Think of me as your Panic Sommelier: I pick the brand of panic that best complements your level of desperation, your tastes in men, and any fatty fish.

1. Better Body Gym, the lowest-priced gym in town, where you've worked out for two years at prime PF-spotting times and sporting the most flattering outfit known to spandex, has helped you score neither sleeker thighs nor a PF. You:
   a Seek out the only guy who's pursued you at the gym—Gary, the pharmaceutical salesman—when he's visibly struggling with the weights, knowing full well you can bench-press the scrawny little pill pusher.
   b Book two back-to-back "Buff Bride" exercise classes, hoping the karma will rub off on you from the germ-laden yoga mat.
   c Take a thousand dollars you can't afford to take out of your 401(k) and upgrade to the trendy three-hundred-dollar-a-month L.A. Sports Club for only three months, the amount of time you're allotting yourself to land more suitable, and wealthy, marriage material. And apply the remaining hundred dollars to a personal training session so said marriage material won't be more interested in your personal trainer than you.

2. You're a staunch Democrat who'd even pay to see a Ben Affleck movie just to show solidarity with the left-leaner. But you just had to suffer through an excruciatingly tedious e-mail play-by-play about the surprise engagement of your friends while vacationing in Bora Bora (isn't that annoying?).

   a On a first date with a great guy he mentions how he could never be in a relationship with a liberal, at which point you tell him he just saved you from suffering through a date with a feeble-minded conservative.

   b You crash the next Young Republicans' chapter meeting in a party-line-crossing metaphor for the Panic Years, hoping to make purple babies one day with some khaki-clad "compassionate conservative."

   c If the Young Republicans fete is a bust, you hop over to the Iran Nuclear Arms Humanitarian fund-raiser in search of deep-pocketed PFs. Hey, an activist is an activist!

3. You have to work late and miss an event called "The Flirt Fete," a benefit for Katrina Relief–slash–singles mixer. You:

   a Figure you'll just attend the next event.

   b Run to call your best friend to grill her about the guys in attendance.

   c Research how much longer hurricane season is— maybe you can squeeze in another benefit when the next national disaster strikes.

4. Your roaring twenties are becoming a distant memory, much like any recollection involving human physical contact. You'll take your eggs:

   a Scrambled.

   b Preferably not all over your face, as the last PF you told everyone you were going to marry dumped you at the six-month mark.

   c Frozen in a cryopreservation lab until you get married, hoping they last that long.

5. If you're sobbing and catch yourself saying, "I can't wait 'til I'm dead" in an especially alarming way today, it's because:

   a Your beloved great-aunt died and you're nowhere to
     be found in the will.

   b It's Sunday and you're watching *The Notebook* on
     DVD—it was fated that Allie would be reunited with
     Noah.

   c At the bank you were forced to wait an agonizing fif-
     teen minutes behind some unworthy newlywed who
     signed up for her new joint checking account with
     her less-than-thrilled new husband, while you were
     there simply hoping to waive the penalty fee for a
     bounced check (because if you could afford to pay the
     penalty fee, then you'd have enough money in your
     checking account in the first place, right?).

6. You just broke up with your PF. Your new ring-tone song
is the whistle only a panicker can hear:

   a "I Will Survive"

   b "One Is the Loneliest Number"

   c "99 Ways to Die"

7. Your friend calls you to go out to a party tonight. Your new
policy is to emerge from home only if:

   a You get assurances there will be plenty of desserts.

   b You get assurances that the men outnumber the
     women by a ratio of four to one.

   c They can find someone at this hour with a crane and
     serious tubs of butter to squeeze your lazy, reluctant
     body through the door—then you'll think about it.

8. You're at a restaurant in your usual Panic-driven malaise
when the waitress comes over for your order. "What do
you want?" she grunts. You respond:

   a "Oh, just a fruit salad, thanks. I'm trying to stay slim."

b "Cheese fries would really hit the spot—it's not like anyone will notice if I gain a few pounds."

c "There's nothing physical that you can bring me. What I really need can't be called up from your deep fryer, nor can it be solved by pounding chocolate milk shakes, although I guess you're still testing that theory, aren't you, Margaret? What I need is the intangible, almost imperceptible. What I need is a PF—got that on the menu, sweetheart?"

9. You : Panic Years is as
  a Tolstoy : brevity
  b Morning talk shows : unforced banter
  c You : Panic Years

10. You've just gotten your college alumni magazine in the mail and your former classmates are wreaking havoc on your level of happiness yet again. It was bad enough during those plumper days of dining hall Sloppy Joe taunts, but now they're getting married just to piss you off. You:
  a Cancel your subscription to that smut. You need to read more palatable news, something more upbeat like the *Kabul Gazette.*
  b Submit your own wedding announcement. And while you're at it, why not add that you're now a doctor of neurosurgery? The Gamma-cubed-eating-disorder whores can go fuck themselves!
  c Figure you still have time to crash the wedding of your "Little Sister" and announce the fake one-night stand you had with the groom in your undergrad days. You couldn't stand to see those sorority witches happy then, and it kills you even more to see they've married into money now!

11. When was the last time you had a rollicking good belly laugh?
   a During one of the *Golden Girls* marathons that the good folks at Lifetime are generous enough to supply nearly 24/7.
   b When some seventeen-year-old miniature wunderkind figure skater spun out of her triple axel during tense international competition.
   c When you found out that your vile bride-to-be friend who boasts about getting flowers from her fiancé every Friday (only because she forces him to buy her flowers every Friday) just got dumped (and ironically there was not one sympathy bouquet to be found).

12. How old were you the last time you said, "It's so much fun to go to weddings!"?
   a Twenty-three.
   b My friends stopped inviting me to weddings.
   c When the hell would I have ever said that?

13. What was the last bad lie you told?
   a "I really love being single and having time for me right now."
   b "I'm so happy for my best friend, who got engaged, that I don't even feel any jealousy!"
   c "Did you hear about the newlyweds who died in that tragic skydiving accident? Real shame . . ."

If you answered mostly As, you're a Serial Single but Stable. You valiantly sit at the singles table at your friends' weddings with unfaltering poise. You've flown solo for New Year's Eve for the past two years—bravely weathering advances from trashed Eurotrash tourists at Times Square with aplomb—and

as of now your only prospect of a PF is a third cousin once re-
moved who's supposedly getting out of a relationship. But
somehow, with the tides of the Panic lapping at your ankles,
you manage to keep your head above water and find the silver
lining in your singleness. Just proceed with caution—you
never know when a tsunami will hit!

If you answered mostly Bs, you're Borderline Bitter. You
sad little sack of single—all these love handles without the
love. Where's the justice in the high court of dating? You feel
like you're walking on the panic plank—and jumping in
means literally being eaten by the love sharks. You're about five
bridesmaid dress fittings away from Panic and there's no turning back. Make sure the symptoms are on your mental map so
you'll be able to avoid any pitfalls on your road to the altar.

If you answered mostly Cs, you're a Panicker Par Excel-
lence. You've given new meaning to the term "pig in a blanket," and waddling out of the house to sign for your UPS
delivery of frozen steaks requires undue effort. The Panic
Years are in your blood, to the point where your new official
blood type is P (now a universal donor). Your penchant for
panic should be applauded and studied in textbooks for new
waves of panickers to come. You really are the Panic Years personified—congratulations and now let's kick it for good!

Now that we've established what the Panic Years are and how
to recognize the symptoms, the next critical step is to conquer them—while finding your way to a happy, lasting relationship with a panic-free foundation.

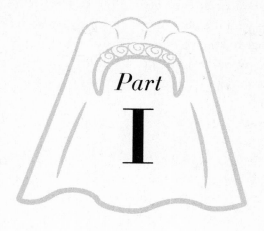

Part

I

Getting Physically and
Psychologically Prepared
for Wedding Warfare:

Boot Camp for the

Bride-to-Be

Part I is designed as an elixir for the woman with Walking Panic Years, which is to say the woman who has all the symptoms of the condition, but no antidote. This section helps you to combat this ailment strategically. Each victory in the battle—such as dropping a toxic friend to let her wallow in her own wasteland of negativity without dragging you down with her—helps you win the greater wedding war.

All the tools for a take-no-prisoners approach to getting married are at the ready, along with strategies to keep your Panic at bay. For instance, do not let the ex who's getting married enter your stream of consciousness, even if wedding day sabotage has more than crossed your mind and crossed over into your court-ordered buffer zone. And don't let the bridesmaid blues grip you—or taint your friendship with the bride.

And for the love of God, no buying cat food in bulk! Hot
guys shop at the supermarket too. Save your self-respect—and
your double coupons—for other locations!

This first section pays homage to the movie every single
girl who's secretly panicked loves to quote from: *When Harry
Met Sally:*

> "All I'm saying is that somewhere out there is the man
> you are supposed to marry. And if you don't get him
> first, somebody else will, and you'll have to spend the
> rest of your life knowing that somebody else is married
> to your husband."

So get ready to venture out into that dating jungle, pull
up those drooping panty hose, poach that poor sap of a PF,
and get those wedding wheels in motion! Remember, there
are two roadblocks to the altar: your lack of commitment and
your conscience—and we have no time to indulge either. So
let's get you through this with aplomb, keeping at least some
of your pride intact, and get you on your married way!

Why You're Never Too Young
to Start Panicking

One traumatic college incident that still haunts me to this day (besides the time a burly, misunderstood linebacker known as RibCracker asked me out) involves a girl named Becky Goodman. Sounds innocuous enough, right? I, too, was fooled by the floral-scented moniker—but after a serious learning curve in Panic, I realized this cupcake was baked in the devil's oven.

Becky, like most two-faced reptiles, was smooth on the outside and a steely predator on the inside, and not a day went by that she didn't work to ensure that image. By the time she turned eighteen, Becky was on a mission to get married. Her unofficial personal mantra: if you're old enough to become resentful of your friends' relationships, then you're old enough to panic. And she wasn't going to let anyone get married be-

fore she did. If you so much as impeded her path in any inad-
vertent way, good luck to you! No one got in Becky's way,
and if you did, you had to be prepared to sleep with one eye
open and sit with your back to the wall for the rest of your
living days.

The campus community at large saw Becky only as a
good-natured coed, but as her sole reptile tamer, I was af-
forded the pleasure of observing her in her natural habitat behind the glass display case. Becky knew that she was going to
be in school for only a few years and therefore had only so
much time to secure The One. With pride she'd regale me
with stories of how her grandmother had operated in the
same aggressive fashion to snag her first husband (who eventually divorced her) and employed the same technique to
marry her second (who also divorced her) and finally to meet
her third husband . . . Becky's dear grandfather—who was
too slow, I presume, to outswim Grandma's fishing line.

One of Becky's first tadpoles was this great guy, Keith,
whom she dated from freshman into sophomore year. Did she
love him? Enough. But when he started getting "too humanitarian" for her liking, Becky knew time wasn't to be wasted
and cut the line, releasing him back into his little middle-class
pond with the rest of the do-gooder guppies. Turns out that
Keith offhandedly mentioned that he wanted to become a
teacher and Becky, after all, as she explained, really needed
someone who understood "the importance of money."

"Some people are all about working hard, but I think life
is about smelling the roses," the White Oleander herself
would reason. "Keith just doesn't come from money—how
would it ever work?" This despite her mom's attempt at bro-
kering unity between the happy couple when she reassured
Becky that when they started a family, she'd pay for a nanny,
"worse come to worse."

This was the thought process of a nineteen-year-old who was preemptively conquering the panic (questionable tactics aside). Now that's foresight! Looking back, I don't know whether to be proud of this bona fide Panic Years product of higher education or ashamed. I think it's a cocktail of both.

Panicked and Proactive—She May Be Ruthless, but She's Not Ringless

After breaking up with Keith, the do-gooder teacher-in-training, Becky swung into advanced Panic Mode. Already a sophomore and starting virtually from scratch, Becky knew she had her work cut out for her. She switched gears on many levels: most notably, she dropped her women's studies major for more PF-friendly, neutral sociology after her mother suggested that women's studies might be construed as "too aggressive"—potentially threatening to the PFs who like their women to know their place. Because when you really think about it, championing the feminist movement and elevating the cause to new dimensions might very well conflict with trying to settle down and land a husband by twenty-two.

Enter, almost on cue, Darren, the guy Becky had sat next to in her freshman-year Politics, Philosophy, and Ethics class (no, the irony wasn't lost on me). In the interest of marrying Future Money, she made sure that Darren was headed to law school and was destined to become one of America's brightest legal bulbs. He was a nice enough guy, according to Becky, even though he'd "prattle on and on about world events."

"I try to feign interest in what he's saying, I try to look attentive, but it's just so boring. I'm wondering how much of this I can take," she'd moan. Was he putting her to sleep with sophomoric frat boy stories of beer pong championships? Or whispering logic theories as mind-benders into her ear? Turns out, it was worse: "He goes on endlessly about how shocking it is that ethnic cleansing still occurs in this day and age—give me a break! I mean, talk about something I care about!"

But his poor conversation skills aside, Becky determined that she would date Darren for the long haul; she set about projecting roses all the time, and never let him see just how tainted that soil was. She masked anything she didn't want Darren to see, angles of her life that she thought would jeopardize their relationship, and, more specifically, threaten the chances of a ring.

And she was successful. She set out to secure a husband in college and a husband she got. He proposed at the end of her senior year. And now they live richly ever after, just the way Becky always dreamed it would be.

So when Becky got a ring for graduation and I got university sweatpants, I knew that the dating divide between the two of us required intensive analysis. From that time on, I've noticed without exception that the girls I know who are getting engaged to the elusive "nice guys" are almost always the Beckys—the-benign-enough-on-the-outside, malignant-on-the-inside, calculating aggressors who know what the goal is and how to go after it.

Why Panicking Young Pays Off

While Becky's antics might seem extreme—and I'm talking "extreme" compared to a religious fundamentalist—she artfully managed to avert future full-throttle panic at a tender age, and you can too. At the heart of Becky's actions lay the deep-seated fear that she would never get married and that very fear became the driving force behind her Olympic-style push for a PF. She didn't succumb to panic, she took action. And as a result, she landed a truly eligible guy while the rest of us were twiddling our thumbs.

Putting marriage on your mental map when you're young makes that destination much easier to reach than starting the journey ten years from now—when full-blown panic infects an otherwise healthy outlook. The truth is it's a lot harder when you start thinking about marriage in your thirties than it is in your twenties; so while you don't have to declare "PF poaching" as a double major in college, like Becky, getting in a serious state of mind for marriage sooner rather than later will help your campaign tremendously—and make dating along the way infinitely more fun!

In this chapter you will learn about the benefits of being marriage minded now (not ten years from now); why doing so can help you avoid full-throttle panic later on and make dating a whole lot less stressful along the way; the realities of an aging SPS; and how to embrace the confidence of your youth.

Set Your Alarmist Clock Now

I'm inviting you to join the program: the pre–Panic Years program, that is. And you won't regret it. It's essentially taking the first fundamental steps on your climb to the altar. Addressing these fears and concerns now will spare you greater dating woe in the years to come. Think of this as your inoculation against an aggressive strain of panic that could infect you years down the line. You're a youngish, delicate flower—but believe me, you will wilt and die from stress and loneliness if you don't take preemptive counterpanic measures now.

Your Stardom—Use It While You've Got It Before It Burns Out

Here's a heads-up for all you reluctant panickers out there: You're not twenty-two anymore. At twenty-two you were a shining star. But, as you're well aware, stars are finite and they're gas—a gas that evaporates into a cloud of infinitesimal dust with time. There are more stars in the sky than grains of sand, which also, incidentally, slip through your fingers like the years of our youth. Stars in their prime (lasting up to a few billion years) are comparable to us at twenty-two—they're hot. Really hot. Showstoppers that could halt traffic. But stars burn out without anyone really noticing, while countless others crop up to take the departed star's place. You were once that shining star—and now you're free-falling through the atmosphere dangerously fast, but you're not off the solar system map just yet.

The lesson here is: use it while you've got it! Sitting at home thinking, "Oh, I'm sure I'll meet someone someday . . ." while listening to your friends talk about *their* dates and *their* lives makes for a life of passivity that has romantic forlornness written all over it. It's a little-known secret that women in their twenties age in two-year increments: twenty-one and promiscuous becomes twenty-three and discriminating. Twenty-three and discriminating becomes twenty-five and crying into a tear-soaked pillow with every friend who gets engaged. And twenty-five and crying into a tear-soaked pillow turns into "Is there even a life worth living anymore?"

Time has a funny way of sneaking up on us, like an ill-timed cold sore on the corner of your lip on New Year's—when it's too late to camouflage and the damage has already taken its heinous toll. And even the best concealer can only cover up, not reverse, the damage. What's made me keenly aware of this phenomenon is watching my elderly single friends (thirty-plus years old) over soft foods and bingo at the home. Much to my chagrin, I've seen these onetime vibrant, beautiful, confident women with the world at their perfectly pedicured feet revert into closed-off self-made "old maids" in the cruelest way of all: with passing time. They've slowly opted out of the whole scene and become disenchanted, figuring "What's the point?"

I've also noticed that a woman's confidence seems to drop precipitously with each failed relationship once she crosses a certain line in her life. If you drop two hundred feet when you're rejected by a guy for another girl your age, imagine the cumulative impact of being rejected by someone for a twenty-six-year-old when you're a few years older and can no longer ignore the signs that you need reading glasses? It's like dropping a thousand feet instead of two hundred feet. Now that's a dose of panic that doesn't go down well. No matter how much mental and emotional mettle you think you possess, rejection like that chips away even at women of Herculean strength of spirit. Your confidence simply droops along with every other erstwhile asset you showboated in your twenties heyday. But it doesn't have to—if you can manage to bypass the panic before it reins you in.

"There's Always More Fish"—A Myth You Need to Overcome

The idea that there will "always be another one looming on the horizon" isn't necessarily a given for those who think they can drink from the endless well of PFs; the reality is that you don't know when your well is going to run dry. I know a woman, Jennifer, who, over the years, would unceremoniously dump guys as cavalierly as, well, a callous guy would—without genuine reason or consideration, instead always assuming, "Oh, there will just be another one." That convenient little nugget served as her internal security blanket every time she'd end a relationship. She never looked back, or at least never admitted to it, and always relied on the limitless number of quality available men. Jennifer is now a dating luminary in her late thirties and in the six years I've known her, her stump speech about there always being another one right around the corner has become less and less convincing. And her personal confidence curve has unfortunately been in free-fall to irretrievable lows.

That's not a cautionary tale you want to be a part of. Trust me.

Similarly, I see other onetime femme fatales' confidence crumble like day-old bread with the passing years. And with each high-quality guy you take a pass on, insisting "I'm not looking right now," believe me, one day you will be and the regret will really sink in. And it's not just that some of us aren't looking, it's that we reject guys for ridiculous reasons—zeroing in on the most arbitrary of factors, like he's too politically conservative, too bald, or even too nice. If you don't stop to think before blithely discarding someone, any woman with a modicum of intelligence will immediately scoop up the ones you left behind. And by the time you realize that he's exactly what you needed, someone less myopic than you will have grabbed him—and carried him over her shoulder all the way to the altar herself.

I've seen women in their thirties and forties with the so-called whole package reduced to decoding and analyzing men's behavior, exhibiting self-doubt, and second-guessing even the most minute details, as if they're sixteen and trying to figure out whether the boy in homeroom likes them. Because at that age, guys are harder to come by, marital pressure is mounting, and the game becomes that much more competitive. It's almost as if their confidence and self-worth come full circle: the thirty-six-year-old feels as clueless and mystified by "men's confusing signals" as the sixteen-year-old. Their confidence isn't just shaken at this point—when unfortunately it's generally harder to find a PF and actually make him stick—it's shattered. But their example doesn't need to send you into the depths of greater panic—yet. Just try to remember not to jeopardize your romantic future of tomorrow by shortchanging a great candidate today.

Men are famously lambasted for the short-sightedness they demonstrate in dating. Are we going to let the inferior sex contaminate our thinking too? We test higher in problem solving and verbal analogies for a reason, ladies: we are the ones who are expected to reason things through before we swiftly decide to discard someone!

What we can learn from our elders

There's no greater moment an SPS can experience—an event so memorable that it prompts a palpable feeling of joy—than when she benefits from the wisdom of elders—grandparents who lived in a world that no stories or pictures can ever convey; old people at the bank who are confounded by the velvet ropes and remember the days when velvet ropes were reserved solely for Studio 54; friends twenty-nine and older whose war stories of dating woe serve as the deepest lesson for any youngster with a stash of bridal mags under her pillow and a dream.

One such sage relic is my friend Vera, whose last days as a twentysomething had her waxing nostalgic while blubbering into her Chipotle nachos during our lunch. She whispered, "When I was twenty-three, I thought I didn't want to get married before I was thirty and that I wanted one kid at thirty-two and the other at thirty-four—tubes tied at thirty-five. Two kids because that's how many fit comfortably in a Mercedes and at restaurant tables. It's scary to be crossing out of the twenties, the career years, and into the thirties, the family years. The party's over when that happens. And here I am, still single, but with two promotions in the last year to justify it. I just didn't realize how many women were out there husband hunting while I was busy getting promoted. And now there are no single men left—everyone I meet is either engaged, attached, or married." At which point she trails off into something inscrutable. But in an instant, she dusts off her ancient frame holding together a weary sack of bones and snaps back to life: "Get out there now before you're twenty-nine and it's too late! If I can't enact my plan, my whole life is shot to hell. You don't want to wind up like me!"

With twenty-twenty hindsight, Vera is only now coming to terms with something she should have addressed a long time ago: that finding a suitable husband doesn't come with the snap of a finger, and starting to search for him at nearly thirty makes things even tougher. Now that her Panic has exploded in volatility, she certainly wishes she hadn't let a decade come and go before she decided to look seriously for a PF. You too should be mindful of time—not obsessed with it—and the search for your own PF will go a lot more smoothly.

Why it's better to panic now than panic later!

If we don't proactively at least try to date for marriage now, then we have no one to blame but ourselves when we're still single down the road. As discouraging as fruitless dating can sometimes be, it's the only way to mine your way through the pack to find your perfect guy. Over a lifetime, we're bound to confront many regrets—don't make waking up one day in your late thirties and wishing that you dated more seriously and actively in your twenties one of them. So use your panic to your advantage and make it the motivating force that gets you out there.

Remember: the Panic Years do not discriminate—whether you're twenty-two and clinging to hope or thirty-one and clinging to life, Panic knows no bounds.

Panic by Proxy

Even if your panic is in short supply, your family's isn't. Do any of the following scenarios trigger a sudden rash and/or burning sensation?

- Your mom cases the joint at weddings—slipping your number to the minister, hoping he'll keep a lookout for the cute single guys. "What's wrong with a little shopping for men at weddings? I'm my Amy's only marriage watchdog!" she innocently postures.
- You've caught yourself saying, "No, not everyone needs a date for New Year's Eve, Mom. Yes, I know there's a small but distinct possibility that there could

be a terrorist incident and this would be my last chance to kiss someone."
- You're lazily reading the paper one day when you see an ad for a "White Hot Elephant Sale," and for a split second you suspect that your mom has placed a singles' ad on your behalf.
- For her birthday, your mom passive-aggressively asks for the book *How to Marry Off Your Kids.*
- You're an accomplished molecular biologist conducting groundbreaking research at twenty-eight and your twenty-four-year-old sister still has to sound out "con-science" to spell it correctly. Yet, she was pelted with "I'm so proud of you!" droplets when she got married while you were rained on by Dad's disgusted "You couldn't bring a date?" dig at your Ph.D. graduation.

If any of these scenarios have you inexplicably curled up in a fetal position and listlessly muttering, "I am dating someone seriously, Mom, I promise," then you likely have a parent—or two—who is projecting their insidious Panic by Proxy onto you. Panic by Proxy is to unmarried women what Kryptonite was to Superman—an assault that erodes your core of contentment until you become a mere shell of your former self. Panic by Proxy is the unrelenting (and self-defeating) pressure that family members and especially fidgety parents project onto you: the unmarried black sheep tarring your family's good name.

The anxiety and nervousness that your parents harbor about their knitted baby booties for future grandchildren getting mothballed and their status with their friends at the club, and possibly even your own happiness, trickle down to infect your outlook on your marital timeline, sending your own panic sky high. Sure, most of the time they just tease and pester about your single status, but occasionally you get that card in the mail from Mom that you can't wait to open—until you discover that it's a newspaper clipping about the spike in suicides among lonely single women.

Why does the Panic cloud their clarity and transform otherwise loving parents into unbearable interrogators when it comes to your nuptial status? They say they do it for love (wasn't that Jeffrey Dahmer's defense?). They "want only what's best for you," and to them that means getting you happily hitched and out of the house. True, they may justifiably fear you've hit rock bottom after being placed on a Girl Scout security watch list for calling the headquarters seventeen times demanding to know when cookie season starts, but the cookie isn't the only thing that's crumbling here: your very sanity is on the brink when your family is breathing down your neck about why you're *still* single. And despite their good intentions, they are nevertheless culpable for deepening your singles' "mea culpa."

Why they put such exquisite focus on you getting married is simple: now that their personal life goals are met and they've finished reaching for their own stratospheric stars, all their energy is deposited onto you. Unfortunately, their reality is often so clouded that they can't see past what *they* want for you to accept what you want for yourself. As all of the following examples amply demonstrate, some parents are so consumed with getting their kids married off—projecting all their long-held marital dreams onto us, the next generation— that they are literally left with no sense of how this pressure is affecting the very children they are trying to help.

Real-Life Proxy—The Worst Offenders

"The pressure really started in high school, when my mom would grill me about dating," recalls Nina, twenty-nine. "At my sweet sixteen party, my mom saw two of my friends kissing and she became resentful that I wasn't with anyone. From that day on, she basically hasn't stopped nagging me about why I'm not dating anyone."

Nagging, it seemed, graduated quickly to nitpicking and nitpicking erupted into derision. "After that, every time I bit my nails or let my eyebrows become 'too ungroomed,' she'd get on my case about my habits; about how no one would marry me if he heard me chew my gum so loudly and other things of that nature. The most self-conscious I ever got was when she constantly criticized the hair on my arms." Under her mother's unforgiving microscope and after one too many demoralizing criticisms, Nina finally caved and waxed her arms to get Mom off her back. But she reacted violently to the wax, which left her arms in wrenching pain for days.

"Then, in junior year of college," Nina goes on, "as soon as she met my new boyfriend, she wanted me to accelerate the relationship and steer it onto a more serious course. Of course I subconsciously rebelled and instead put on the brakes and ended it with him. It's a shame, because he was a really nice guy and who knows, maybe it could have lasted, but her pressuring was just too much—I lost the ability to let the relationship evolve naturally. And look where I ended up." Fifteen years later, the rhetoric hasn't really changed. "I recently found this in my mailbox: *We live in a couples world— you better get with the program or you'll be left alone. (Happy Birthday, Love, Mom and Dad . . .)*" Today, Nina is still single, and her mom has only herself to thank.

But Panic by Proxy doesn't always start when you're young, and it can even surface in the most unlikely of places. "My mom was always an advocate of me living my life," Christine, twenty-eight, told me. "She always told me to travel, be independent, and live my life for myself 100 percent. Then I turned twenty-six and all of that was suddenly shot to hell. Now I have to screen her calls most of the time because I can't stand listening to her bemoaning my being single."

The greatest danger of Panic by Proxy is that it can hinder us from making decisions that we know deep down are right for ourselves. Mandi was thirty and about to call off her engagement to a man who left her with malnutrition to the heart. Her mom came through with her interpretation of support: "Are you sure you want to do this, sweetie? This could be your last chance to get married!"

But Mandi's gut feelings eventually won out over her mother's griping, and even though the planning was well under way, she finally found the courage to call off the wedding and has never felt better. Her mother hasn't fared so well. "Oh, my poor mother," Mandi says. "All she can bring herself to say to me now is 'Well, I hope you're happy—all the guys your age are taken!' and throw up her hands in resignation."

Home Is Where the Panic Is

The expression goes, "You can't pick your parents." But has anyone ever asked the truly essential question: "Can you at least pick your parents' meds?" Besides nudgy parental panickers, my extended family has swelled into a full Panic by Proxy posse—aunts, cousins, and other relatives, all of whom are unabashedly (and vocally) disturbed by my single status.

It seemed as though the ominous cloud hanging over my

head had been lifted—if only momentarily—a few years ago when I started dating someone. At the time, my older sister had been in a serious relationship and my aunt's rosy projections could not be contained, hinting at a possible double wedding for me and my sister. Well, my aunt got half her wish—my sister married her boyfriend but I disappointingly couldn't scare up a groom in time to make it a double feature. I mean, with the rabbi and reception hall already rented for the day, it was almost stupid not to get married right then and there! After all, when are my hair and makeup ever going to look that polished again?

Panic usually starts in families because they are the epicenter of both nosiness and concern. Unfortunately, they are also usually the people you can't escape, even if you want to. Panic is also known to be passed from generation to generation like a bad gene: a panicked mother in the New World probably resulted from a panicked grandmother from the old country and will in turn probably transform you into a first-class panicker yourself. It's a cycle that can seem very hard to break.

Susan, fifty, is freshly divorced, and now her mother relentlessly nags her about when she's going to get *remarried*. "She's seventy-five and she won't leave me alone! She yells about how attractive I still am; that I still have the figure of a forty-year-old! That I'm wasting my best years! She said the same thing to me thirty years ago!" Says Susan's mom: "You don't think you're ready to get remarried, but you are! You keep thinking you're going to look like this forever—but you're not! You think you're always going to have your teeth?"

"Of course I'd never do that to my own daughter," insists Susan, "who, much to her own detriment, still insists that her career is making her truly happy and refuses to invest in a relationship now. Now what's wrong with her dating a little instead of fixing lightbulbs and defragging computers on the weekend? Not that I would stick my nose in . . ."

And yet, when I ask her about the women of my generation, she's quick to voice her opinion. "These girls are in denial. They don't acknowledge that they're getting older. There are always going to be girls who are prettier, thinner, smarter, richer—you have to start looking now. They can't admit that time is moving on. You don't know what life has to offer—grab! There are people who claim to want to be alone—I don't buy it! Everyone needs someone—it's a couples world, for both genders! You look at a little squirrel and it's looking for a mate. I don't think there's a living thing on this earth that isn't looking for a mate. You have your whole life for a career, now is your time to get a husband. These girls don't think they're ready to get married, that they're not responsible enough—but they're wrong!"

The apple doesn't fall far from the tree, does it?

Passing the Panic Baton

Another unfortunate side effect of Panic by Proxy is its infectiousness beyond immediate family circles. If you think you're in the clear because your parents have been on mute while your best friends' parents have become the Panic Police, consider yourself warned: the baton is forever passed from proxy to proxy. The Panic is contagious. Miraculously, as soon as the kid of your parents' friends gets married, the panic is automatically transferred from those parents to your own: "Now *we're* not the only ones in the neighborhood whose children aren't married—you are!" our neighbor singsonged gleefully to my parents. If it weren't for that fractured hip, you know he would have done Olympic-worthy cartwheels down the block.

A girl I worked with, Nikki, twenty-four, described the Panic that immediately started spreading when she got engaged. Even though her parents had never been especially panicked, what followed was a massive chain reaction. "My aunt came up to me at my wedding—I thought she was coming in for a heart to heart, to dispense some last-minute advice—and instead asked if I wouldn't mind talking to my older cousin Ryan about proposing to his longtime girlfriend—during my wedding! As soon as I got engaged, that's when it started. All my parents' friends went crazy and started pressuring their own kids.

"Now, every single mah-jongg session is like a singles-by-extension clinic. Every mom is trying to set up her son and daughter during the game. So one mom is telling her son to check out her friend's daughter on Facebook, where the daughter has a profile, screaming wildly, 'She's perfect for you!' One mom even hacked her way onto her son's Match.com account to doctor his profile from "interested in dating" to "interested in marriage and kids" without his knowledge. And she's taking way too many liberties with the winks.

What You Can Do to Cope—Proactive Strategies to Help You Get Results

The outlook may seem bleak now—as your parents are spending their declining years steeling themselves from the grim reality that you're still single and are starting to show signs of lost hope. But luckily there are tools you can use to dodge Panic by Proxy and salvage those last shreds of your sanity.

STRATEGY #1: Move Out on Your Own

Adrienne is twenty-nine and a haughty WMD (Witless Married Dullard), but she didn't reach this milestone without taking a few instrumental measures to minimize the Panic by Proxy side effects. Living under her parents' roof—and by extension, under their thumb—exacerbated Adrienne's own fears and, apparently, her parents' social anxieties. "I have nothing to tell my friends! What am I supposed to tell them? I'm embarrassed to see them at this point!" her mom would lament over Adrienne's singleness. "She would actually have her friends sidle up to me in a not particularly subtle way, playing the 'I'm not your mom, I'm your friend—you can tell me anything!' card to try to get the scoop for my mom," Adrienne recalls. That's when she was finally able to see what had been hidden for years: the fact that she needed to move out of the state and far away from her parents—fast. "When a job opportunity came up in Chicago, I jumped at it," she said, "and I think it was the first time I could hear myself think and actually date someone without the mandatory daily debriefings that were making me crazy and unsure about my own priorities."

If your parents are hovering, try striking out on your own. Putting some distance, and that psychological buffer, between yourself and them has tremendous benefits for your mental—and your dating—health.

STRATEGY #2: What They Don't Know Won't Hurt Them

There's still one thing worse in this world than being temporarily unhitched, and that's being unhinged—and Meghan was well on her way to being both, thanks to her mom's persistent Panic. She feared that her mom's pestering might not just destroy her own sanity, but could threaten her longtime relationship with her boyfriend, Justin, who endured constant

PALO ALTO CITY
LIBRARY

Rinconada Library
1213 Newell Road
Palo Alto, CA 94303
(650) 329-2436 .
http://webcat.cityofpaloalto.org
==================================

Items that you checked out

Title: "When did you see her last?" /
ID: 31185013645488
Due: Wednesday, October 14, 2015

Total items: 1
Account balance: $3.70
Wednesday, September 16, 2015 6:36 PM

New Hours Coming After Labor Day 2015!!
See: http://bit.ly/1InytT8

Service Note: Self-Check Machines now
require you PIN input for secure Transactions.

interrogations about his marriage intentions from his would-be mother-in-law. "I couldn't take my mom's nagging anymore. I had been dating Justin for two years and it was driving my mother crazy that I was already twenty-seven and we weren't engaged yet."

Before Meghan's visit home for a birthday, she knew showing up without a ring would taint the mood of the entire weekend, so she became very resourceful. "When I was planning my trip home, I knew that if I wasn't engaged by the time I saw her, it would be a weekend of more nagging hell. So I got a fake ring for twenty bucks just to shut her up. It actually worked and it turned into a really great visit!" But what about Justin? Three months later, when the next visit home for the holidays rolled around, Meghan had a *real* ring to show off. He proposed at Christmas and her mother never knew! Buying herself some extra time so her mom wouldn't have a meltdown was the best thing she could have done for herself—and her relationship.

Sometimes we need to get our parents off our backs—by any means necessary—for our own sanity and peace of mind. In the end, what they don't know won't hurt them, so exercise your right to keep the play-by-play of your relationship as private as possible.

STRATEGY #3: Confront Them—Once and for All

Remember, Panic by Proxy is like a hideous perm gone awry: the problem won't fix itself. Another effective strategy is to confront the familial offenders head on and explain that their projected pressure on you is crushing your self-esteem and putting an undue strain on your relationship. You want a PF, they want you to have a PF, so if you both want the same thing, why belabor the point? Point out that not only are their outbursts backfiring, but their thoughtless comments are cutting you deeply with every insensitive jab, compounding a situation you don't need to make worse.

Kristen, thirty-one, remembers a time when her dad's Panic by Proxy slowly clogged her breathing. She recalls how crushed she was when she broke up with a boyfriend and all her dad did to soothe her pain was to coat her emotional wounds with salt. "All he said was 'Oh, that's a shame! Twenty-five is such a perfect age to get married.' It was not helping," she recalls wistfully. When she finally confronted him—admitting that his pressure was actually pushing her away, making her feel *less* inclined to share anything with him—Kristen's dad finally realized he had stepped over the line: "I remember he apologized and said, 'Honey, it's just that I'm so happy to be married that I wish I did it sooner. I just want you to get married too and enjoy what Mom and I have.'" Once Kristen and her dad made amends and were able to speak the same language again, the whole family enjoyed a panic-free future.

In the end, sure, saying that your family marginalizes you like no one else can is like saying John Nash is a guy who knows how to add. They can easily transform your already swelling panic into a condition that is much more acute with just one inquiry to the Alaskan cruise director about the single available men on board physically fit enough to participate in the Ping-Pong tourney. These are presumably the same people who gave you life; now, they're the ones essentially draining you of it. You're almost hoping some cousin comes out of the closet and takes the heat off you for the time being.

But now you have the tools to identify and diffuse this Panic by Proxy phenomenon. And look on the bright side: the sooner you get married, the sooner you can terrorize your own kids with indoctrinated feelings of panic. The circle of life—it's a beautiful thing!

3

Getting Through the Holidays Unmarried and Unscathed

The weather's getting cold. That unmistakable smell of winter is in the air—no more having to take romantic sunset beach strolls with your mom, but now you get to watch lovebirds skating on a frozen lake locked arm in arm. They break into that giddy laugh, as only lovers can, with her every klutzy, uncoordinated fall; ah, if only that ice were a little thinner! It's only natural to resent these hollow expressions of "love" during this, the most ego-eroding of times: the holidays. Suddenly you're faced with a slew of party invitations that beg for dates; that annoying sprig of mistletoe that someone hangs at your company fete; and the inevitable giddy and grating news that another friend popped the question on New Year's Eve. We see other presumably happy couples color coordinated and we just want those red and green twin sets for ourselves. What's a panicker to do?

Yes, the holidays can shine an especially harsh light on the Panic. You're hoping that the store has enough garland so you can spell out P-A-N-I-C on your living room wall, and all you want to do is anesthetize yourself with tryptophan until February 15. Our hearts are buried in a decidedly deep winter during the holidays, and there's even less motivation to shave your legs now than there was when it was actually warm out. But in fact, the holidays can be prime hunting season for PFs if you're clued in to the right strategies.

Engineering strategies, of course, vary from religion to religion, unmarried to unmarried, but the basic tenets of holiday survival are universal. Here's what you can do to abate the panic, beat it, and bring back a PF in time for the really big jewelry sales.

STRATEGY #1: Wipe the Mothballs off That Shamefully Tight Cocktail Dress and Crash Any Holiday Party You Can

This may be the only time of year when men feel more lonely and desperate than you do—or at least on a par with your dating woes. Do not forgo this rare opportunity to prey on the weak. So grab that little black body-skimming cocktail dress that I'm sure fit you at one point and get on that holiday party circuit! No one's checking company IDs at the doors at these things, so piggyback onto your friends' work festivities to get a firsthand look at the coworker your friend Beth swears is perfect for you. There's a guaranteed open bar, guaranteed men—dateless-for-New-Year's-Eve-and-lonely men!—and the odds of finding a PF are in your favor when they're this vulnerable. Just make sure not to throw back too many eggnogs and make a toast in front of the entire company vowing to increase sales by 20 percent next year (impressive for a girl who doesn't even work there . . .).

If trying to tweeze a stubborn nipple hair doesn't sound

like a promising jump start to the Christmas season, I don't know what does. It was at this "a-ha" moment for Crystal, thirty, that she finally smartened up and became proactive about her singles slump. Instead of intently grooming herself and watching reruns on SoapNet, she decided to listen to her best friend, Wendy, who dispensed the precious advice only annoying engaged best friends can give: "Why would you rather watch *One Life to Live* all night instead of actually living your life?" And with that, Crystal knew what she had to do: "I decided to take up Wendy on her invitation to her company holiday party." While Crystal may have felt like a veritable Eliza Doolittle when she enlisted Wendy to help her prep—"Wendy was like this Higgins, primping me in this mini–finishing school because she really wanted me to meet someone, and I was in desperate need of a makeover," laughs Crystal—her overnight grizzled-to-gorgeous transformation won the attention of a colleague of Wendy's, who spotted Crystal elbowing her way to the dips and chips and was charmed. She might not have mastered the Eliza Doolittle comportment by the end of the night, but Crystal's unique style won her a date— and a one-year courtship that's still going strong!

Even if you don't think you're in a party mood—and the idea of vegging and tweezing in your sweats sounds like the most appealing option for the evening—it's easy to flip your mental switch and muster that party face in time for the annual holiday bash (with a little encouragement from a trusted, if not annoyingly persistent, friend). I guarantee it will be more scintillating than watching dusty episodes of soaps all night, and might even lead you to your PF.

How to maximize the number of holiday parties attended:

- Drop heavy-handed hints for invites to your neighbors, hairdresser, personal trainer, and anyone else who has the inside scoop on all the A-list parties with only the A-list hotties.

- Work those industry connections—now is the time for a little client outreach for extra invites . . .
- Eavesdrop at every elevator, treadmill, or water cooler that you can, hoping to glean some info on upcoming fetes.
- Offer to accompany shy girlfriends so they won't have to go solo to their annual office parties—and let flirtations flow as freely as the Cristal.
- For the panicker with a little moxie, you and a girlfriend could crash a holiday party in progress at the local bar or restaurant. Squeeze past security when they get distracted by some socialite's ear-numbing Chihuahua and maybe you can end up with the ultimate party favor—a PF!
- If other people's parties aren't working out, organize your own! (Just be sure to block the e-vite guest list so that the guys will never see the disproportionate male-female ratio!)

STRATEGY #2: Take a Chance on Work Romance

The holidays are the one time of year you can feel empowered to go after that crush you've been harboring. If your burning crush on Jack in accounting has amounted to nothing more than stolen glances as he collates, then make good on this opportunity at the company holiday party to break the bantering ice. The party lighting will undoubtedly be more flattering than the fluorescent lights at your coworkers' birthday parties in the office kitchen. And even if nothing comes of it and Jack decides he wants to spend this New Year's alone with the Xerox, you can still hold your perfectly coiffed head up high and blame it on a bad batch of eggnog.

Have we learned nothing from Laura Linney's coura-
geous overtures in *Love Actually*?

Ways to approach a coworker crush:

- When you hear that his plans to fly home for the
  holidays have been canceled, take the opportunity
  and invite him to the New Year's bash at your best
  friend's place. He'll appreciate your thoughtfulness
  and, if his feelings mirror yours, will jump at the
  chance for some out-of-office face time.
- For months you've walked by that postcard on his
  desk of Rockefeller Center at Christmastime. Now's
  your chance to invite him to ice skate there. Even if
  your current small talk puts you in linguistic Ice Ca-
  pades territory, watching each other clumsily skate
  and fall could be the perfect icebreaker to put you at
  ease.
- If you're really feeling intrepid, leave him a candy
  cane on his desk with a flirtatious note. It could give
  him just the cue he needs to work up the courage to
  ask you out.

STRATEGY #3: Help Those Even More Needy Than Yourself (a Christmas Miracle in Its Own Right)

Old folks' homes and retirement communities depend on the
good graces of volunteers to help make the holidays a little
brighter for the elderly by spending time with the residents.
Sound like the repository for the soft-foods-only set? Perhaps. But for the creative panicker, it's the unspoiled men's
meadow where your lamb awaits—either they're genuine do-
gooders or they're just as surreptitious as you are, in which
case you connivers are cut from the same cloth! But seriously,
there's bound to be at least some cute grandsons visiting the

nursing home who are most likely due to see some sort of financial inheritance soon. Even if you don't meet anyone who'll propose on the spot (besides a few random residents who want to bring you to the American Legion Veterans' Ball—veterans of '49, that is), you can always ask the seniors to tell you their stories about meeting their spouses; all those sweet tales from an era long forgotten can warm even the frostiest of hearts.

Beth, thirty-five, reluctantly signed up to deliver hot meals to the elderly over the holidays last year—only the friend who was supposed to go with her came down with a last-minute flu. Turns out, that raging fever was the best thing to happen to Beth. She was teamed up with Jonathan, who was a regular meals-on-wheels volunteer and, apparently, just Beth's type. By the following year, Beth had to tell her friend she already had a partner for the meals-on-wheels volunteer day—her husband-to-be.

Other friendly "do-gooder" venues for meeting your PF:

- Try volunteering at a festive holiday event organized at your local church or synagogue. Church-hop your holy ass off this holiday, you pious panicker.
- Do some Santa-letter writing at your local community center for needy children. You know any guy you'll meet here has a heart. And while you're delighting children with warm and fuzzy Santa cheer, you might be ho-ho-ho-ing all night long with one of Santa's hottest helpers.
- Find the closest Red Cross building project and show up ready to work. There are bound to be plenty of men there who are good with a hammer and looking for someone to massage those tired muscles.

Surviving Holiday Family Gatherings

Family reunions during the holidays are always a crapshoot. They can either lift the dark cloud hanging over you because you're single and no one is going to see your ho-ho-ho-y "naughty or nice" lingerie this year, or they can soon remind you of the reason you come home only once a year: you don't need your family pointing out how alone you are.

The last time your Aunt Roz tried to foist an inappropriate PF onto you, the director at the funeral home unceremoniously interrupted, asking that all Grandpa Fred's close relatives move into another room before the burial service. "We'll talk about this later," she assured you. But now Christmas dinner with the entire family is back on and so is Roz's crusade to get you hitched. This time, Roz may have made lightning strike: he's forty-one and divorced—the kids live with the mom in Russia—works as a mover, and is "the sweetest thing in the world."

Don't let overzealous relatives crush your otherwise cheery holiday mood. The best way to prevent family members from dampening your spirits, short of muzzling them with that multipurpose Christmas stocking, is give back as good as you get. You can simply suggest that this gem of a guy may be better suited for Roz's own recently divorced daughter. That should shut up Roz long enough for you to enjoy the holidays and savor the time with your less abrasive family members.

Simple remedies to get you through family gatherings unscathed:

- Arrange for a rendezvous with long-lost friends from high school at your town's local pub, where, sadly, you're not IDed at the door anymore. It will give you a chance to hear about how your friends are getting divorced because their parents pushed them into marriage too young. Besides, you never know which forlorn high school computer dork who took his sister to the prom may now be czar of his own tech empire.

- Plan a retro evening of ice-skating or sledding, reminiscent of your pre-panic days—ah, that was the life.
- Don't balk when your mom asks you to accompany her to the mall for some last-minute shopping. Instead, be on the lookout for struggling PFs at the perfume counter. You may be able to help him pick out the perfect gift for Mom (dare I say your future mother-in-law?). Or, walk into the electronics store and affect your best bewildered expression—men will flock to the damsel in electronics distress within thirty seconds, especially if you position yourself next to the new iPhone display.

Other Panic-Inducing Holidays— and How to Enjoy Them

February on Trial

When Valentine's Day rolls around, it's the SPS vs. St. Valentine. It's a private, panic-laced rage that has spurred the war, and most of us don't know how to wage it. You're feeling so demoralized now that when a plate you drop shatters, you just leave yourself a Post-it to "avoid shards of glass in kitchen" because you're too depressed to clean it up. After all, there are only so many affectionate couples you can give dirty looks to on the subway while muttering, "If you're so in love, why can't one of you spring for a cab?" just loud enough for them to hear and shift seats away from you. So how can you turn these Valentine's blues around?

Even if you feel like you have no choice but to officially declare February an affront to all SPSs, just remember that it is only one commercially hyped day. Go to bed early, and by the time you wake up from a restful slumber, it will be February 15—the day all the really good candy sells for half price! If you can't make yourself impervious to the annual unrelenting V-Day campaign for love, here are a few suggestions to help you get through it:

- Still have that spa gift certificate from Christmas? There's no better time to treat yourself to a champagne-caviar facial while all the other unenlightened SPSs are crying their eyes out over cheap beer and stale KitKats.
- Watch all your TiVo-ed episodes of Oprah—you'll be swimming in self-love and acceptance in no time.
- Since this is not an ideal day for PF hunting, initiate a group dinner at your favorite restaurant with some girlfriends—the anti-panic party where you can get a little tipsy and not have to worry about morning-after embarrassment.

Presidents' Day

Every store in America is celebrating and you have no one with whom to check out the sales. To make matters worse, every mattress in the entire country is 60 percent off—and the only person you could possibly share your bed with is your mother when she comes to visit. Although seemingly benign, coming on the heels of the dreaded fourteenth of February, the Presidents' Day burst of pride can make you want to scream.

So instead of wasting your time licking your wounds over a rare three-day weekend, grab some friends and hit the slopes for a little ski and sun. And under all those bulky layers of ski clothes, no black diamond PF will even notice the extra weight you put on from the February 15 candy massacre.

Fourth of July

Our nation's birthday can translate to a panicker's near demise. Any holiday that involves your uncle rubbing suntan lotion on your back in lieu of a PF is not a holiday worth suspending alternate-side-of-the-street parking, in my opinion. If the thought of another Fourth of July watching fireworks with your extended family and a pack of petrified four-year-olds is one you simply cannot bear, I recommend jumping the Fourth of July shark and avoiding this holiday altogether.

How? Circumvent the fireworks and forced family fun by jaunting off to our fashionable but feckless neighbors to the right—bank, that is, as in Paris. Can you think of anything more intoxicating than spending July in Paris? Consult their national calendar beforehand, though, as you don't want to inadvertently book a trip coinciding with Bastille Day—same as Independence Day, but with annoying accents. This may be your only chance to pick up foreign PFs in jeans tighter than your own at outdoor cafés! If Paris isn't your thing, capitalize on the cheap airfares and head north to Canada or south to

Mexico; there's never been a better time to go have an adventure abroad! Vive la Panic!

Joyous national celebrations, spiritually elevated religious observances, and emotionally charged commemorations—it's the worst, isn't it? There really is nothing more depressing than unbridled holiday spirit and the happily coupled who buy complementary paper plates to commemorate it. Just remind yourself, though, that the most egregious holidays come around only once a year and, like your annual trips to the gynecologist, really play out much worse in your mind.

Many of these holiday events seem purposely magnified just to deepen our panic. But this is an excellent opportunity to assert your strength—as a single and as a person—and really try to block out all the negative stimulation with which we're faced. So let these holidays not mark our failure at coping as singles, but rather celebrate our personal mettle and independence.

4

How Not to Be Bitter at Your Friends' Weddings

"Why is everyone less attractive than me getting married and I'm not?!" This, or some variation of it, crosses the mind of every SPS whose less desirable friend ties the knot before she does. Isn't it strange how all of the friends getting married suddenly become classified as hideous charity cases in our warped minds? Is deriding our friends really what we must resort to in order to validate ourselves? Yes, of course it is!

This chapter looks at how you can accept—not fight—the reality of your friends getting married; the fine art of faking (and feeling!) joy at your friends' weddings; and how to cope with the humiliation of wearing a peach organza nightmare whose alterations sapped the last of your meager savings.

Never Let Them See You Scowl

We're all too familiar with that one emotional basket case of a friend who bawls as soon as she sets foot into the cocktail hour, causing the ice sculpture to melt from her satanic aura. Everyone knows that this SPS's crocodile tears of joy are more like tears of jealousy; after all, when her grandmother died, she had the driest eyes in the house—but bring her to a friend's wedding and she's swimming in salty-teared sorrow. Inevitably, her cover will be blown when the photographer zeroes in on her sour expression as the bride walks down the aisle. Check your friends' wedding albums—there's always one scowling, bitter single friend. Don't let this unattractive ball of bitterness become you!

Yes, it's annoying that your permanent status on theknot. com is the unyielding "maid of honor." But instead of imbibing your way through another uninspired bridal shower with punch you've made naughty—a cheerful homage to the bride's school dance days of dalliances—try a different approach. Even if your normal MO is earning the groom's admiration (he emphatically declares you "his kind of people" and challenges you to see who can drink whom under the white linen table), next time try to derive pleasure and genuine happiness from watching your friend enjoy her blindingly pastel shower, saturated with women who invariably affect those fake British accents. As long as you keep your sense of humor and remember that this too shall pass, that sight alone should be enough to make you smile.

**IRKSOME COMMENTS TO IGNORE
AT OTHER PEOPLE'S WEDDINGS:**

- The groom's homely, yet somehow married, sister: "Wow, good for you to be able to be happy at other people's weddings!"
- Some smarmy second cousin on the groom's side makes an offhanded comment while you're trying to focus on inhaling your wedding cake: "Keep eating—I hear it's good luck for single women. Like catching a bouquet!"
- The five-year-old ring bearer: "Why aren't your teeth white?"
- The minister: "Whoa! Do you drink like this even when it's not an open bar?"
- Complacent WMDs making small talk during the cocktail hour: "So, do you have any horrible dating disaster stories?"
- Groom, now with a contract out on him, to the girls-only singles' table: "I would have put my single buddy from college at this table, but I wouldn't want you girls eating him alive."

Picture it: 1972, Chicago suburbs. An effervescent twenty-five-year-old named Sandy is savoring her wedding day, replete with seventies hair, aqua and lavender floral color schemes, and pacifists aplenty. But then: enter the twenty-five-year-old resentful best friend.

"Before the wedding, the photographer came to my parents' house and the family took pictures out in the backyard," Sandy recalls. "When the bridal party was in the room before the wedding, my best friend Nancy made two comments which really upset me. They seem rather ridiculous now, but at the time I was livid! She held up her foot and said her new navy shoes were killing her, which was her surreptitious way of letting me know that her shoes didn't match the rest of the bridesmaids', who were in aqua. But if she had to buy new shoes anyway, why couldn't she just get the aqua ones? The gowns were long and if she hadn't said anything I would never have known. She did it purely to upset me." And you thought you were spiteful . . .

Then, when best friend Nancy was cued into the chapel, just before walking down the aisle, she launched another mean-spirited missile—pointing out a stain on the bride's dress just seconds before the procession began. "It was the worst thing anyone could have done; literally thirty seconds before I was to take my first step. The spot on the back of my gown must have come from taking the pictures in the back-yard. Again, I would never have known about it if she hadn't mentioned it."

The friendship breakup lasted six years until Sandy and Nancy were pregnant at the same time. Now that their own children are in their twenties and one is getting married, both families are hoping history doesn't repeat itself with another standoff. "I did understand that she was really jealous, but I could not get over it at the time," Sandy admits. "We didn't speak until I realized that we had both moved to the same town, both got pregnant at the same time, and our children would be in homeroom together! So I called her and we got together. It was awkward at first, but we had so much of a his-tory that we eventually got over it."

HOW *NOT* TO HELP WITH THE WEDDING PLANNING:

Sandy's wedding checklist:

✓ Something old

✓ Something new

✓ Something borrowed

✓ Something blue in the face (unmarried friend seething with jealousy because she's left in the singles' wasteland of the Chicago area, twenty-five and getting older and more bitter by the second)

Sandy may have found some space in her heart to forgive Nancy's overtly hideous behavior, but your own friends may not be as generous with you. Don't let this kind of bitterness cloud your judgment and risk dissolving a longtime friendship. And don't pit your friend as the enemy—she's not the real enemy here. (Your bridesmaid dress stakes that claim all on its own.) Try to keep it in perspective: one day—albeit a day in a cruel, cruel gown—is not worth losing a friendship. Besides, there are serious repercussions to your resentment and it bleeds directly into your PF prowl; the single guys crawling at weddings can spot your bitterness in a poofy dress a mile off and it's hugely unattractive.

How to Exercise Restraint

When one escapes from the Lexington, Kentucky, community of zombie brides, as Laura, twenty-six, has successfully managed to do, the backlash seems to be subject to no statute of limitations. After having been away from home for more than eight cotillion-free years, living and working as a successful publicist for a lobbying firm in D.C., Laura felt no anxiety in returning to her hometown for a good friend's wedding last year. Her parents, however, were another story; if they were the betting kind, they'd likely have lost the farm miscalculating their daughter's life and marriage goals; why she couldn't tame a nice thoroughbred accountant from a good Kentucky family was beyond them. But even though all her friends had left her in the dust in the race to the altar, Laura still looked forward to seeing one of her closest friends achieve her personal Triple Crown—marriage.

Everything seemed to be running smoothly without any major roadblocks, until the seemingly easiest part—the ceremony. "Normally during Catholic ceremonies," explains Laura, "you offer prayers of petition—you pray for the sick, you pray for the soldiers to return from Iraq safely, you pray for peace." Your run-of-the-mill appeals for a happier world, right? Well, sort of. But at this wedding, the groom's appeal was "We pray for all the single people in the world—that they too can finally find some happiness and true love and get married soon" to a backdrop of three hundred southerners nodding emphatically. (Can I get a hallelujah in the house?!)

"I didn't know what to do," Laura recalls. "As the only single woman there by a margin of fifteen years—what was I supposed to say? Lord, hear our prayer?! I felt so humiliated!" The only thing restraining her from standing up and shouting, "We pray for all the condescending married people to drop dead" was the Southern comportment with which she had been raised. "I wish I could have written my own petition," she says. "How about I pray that married people can actually feel happy and fulfilled! I pray that they don't hide behind their marriage status their whole lives and instead actually live for themselves." But she kept it together and let off all her steam at the bar—the combination of some Southern Comfort and flirting with the cute bartender seemed to do the trick—never for a moment compromising her blue-ribbon manners.

Yes, whether you're a bridesmaid or a guest or the lucky friend selected to do a special solo dance number with the bride's ninety-five-year-old uncle, when you're single, all weddings will push your buttons in some way. But what would seem to be a clarion call to sabotage the rest of their wedding is actually the time to pull it together and exercise your restraint. Even if the haughty bride tries every undercutting trick up her nuptial sleeve to make you crazy, don't take the bait! You are far too resilient to succumb to a few weak one-liners about your single status.

In that spirit, here are some tools to help you feign happiness at your friends' weddings and leave with almost as much grace as you entered:

- Cake + open bar = sugar and booze, and that's always a trusty Band-Aid for wedding day depression.
- Beguiling the cute groomsman in your unspeakable bridesmaid number won't be easy, but your charm and sincere toast to the couple might just do the trick—everyone wants a little wedding nookie.
- When preserving your link in the "Love Train" chain, dig your claws into the bride's shoulders so hard she will see stars.
- When you involuntarily catch the JDate bouquet (yes, such a thing really exists, and no, I don't want to discuss it any further), remember that at least two cameras are rolling, and the still photographer will capture every pixel of your narrowing eyes and

seething glare. So smile like a trooper and just think about what fun you'll have smashing to smithereens the "Drew-Melanie" snow globe that they think is a fun wedding souvenir.

- Pretend that dancing with the five-year-old second cousin who's so dapper in that tuxedo suspender look—while singing, "Just the Two of Us"—is just the thing to tide you over while the bartender's re-stocking.
- Steal more than your share of Godiva chocolate favors—you've earned them!
- "Accidentally" stomp on the bride during the hora; watching her limp, if even momentarily, will be worth it—trust me. There are two hundred people circle dancing—she'll never know it was you. Your panic prints are safe with me.

To Be a Bridesmaid and Live to Tell About It

It's the war story no soldier wants to rehash. No amount of therapy can help with the night terrors. And while you might have lived through it, you certainly don't want to talk about it. It's the Greek tragicomedy known as "the bridesmaid dress" (though clearly in this getup you are no Aphrodite).

Sure, it's a rite of passage, not a personal affront, when the bride sticks you in such hideous garb, but it can still take a serious toll on your emotional well-being—and your wallet. Here are the tell-tale symptoms of a chronic bridesmaid:

- When you hear the word *crinoline,* it induces on-the-spot nausea.

- You feel like it will be impossible to even be in the same room as taffeta for years to come.
- Every time you pass a Williams-Sonoma, you need to breathe into a paper bag.
- You can't come within fifty feet of the word *fuchsia*.
- There's a dartboard with Jessica McClintock on your wall.

If you're shaking uncontrollably right now and/or identifying with three of the above symptoms, you might in fact have been a bridesmaid one too many times. But don't despair—the humiliation and antipathy all dutiful bridesmaids suffer is a universal experience. No one actually *likes* these things, but everyone does eventually bury the resentment, pay off the credit card bill, donate the dress to Goodwill, and move on to live a healthy, normal life.

Attending a bridesmaid dress fitting can register quite low on most people's fun scale, as Annie, twenty-seven, well knows. At the first of five visits to the austere Eastern European seamstress, she was nervous about what was to come. "This tough old biddy with sewing pins in her mouth who was crawling manically on the floor around my hem all of a sudden made a bad day even worse," Annie recalls. The Slavic seamstress with a Commie temperament to match started berating Annie, screaming that she doesn't wear her bra straps tight enough and then intimated that she has been inadvertently contributing to premature saggage for the past fifteen years. But Annie wasn't going to let this tyrant with a sewing machine rattle her. "I decided that instead of letting her get to me, I would just laugh it off. She was a crazy old woman anyway and I wasn't going to lose sleep over it."

But the bridesmaid nightmare didn't end there. Sure, the

word *champagne* sounds like a good thing in theory, but when it's the color of a heinous $450 organza gown that will become your bridesmaid uniform, champagne suddenly sounds very, very bad. The tension was manageable, until the fateful day of the next fitting. The bride, Annie's best friend, matter-of-factly blurted out, "You know you need to lose ten pounds to wear this dress so you won't stand out from the rest of the girls, right?" And that's when the corks started flying. "I think it was at that point that the world heard a collective, 'Oh no she didn't!' "Annie now laughs. "It was one thing to suffer an indirect jab from the seamstress, but to have my best friend give me diet advice, that's where I drew the line. Her expectations were completely out of whack!"

Annie told her friend what her limits were—financially, mentally, and physically—and stood firm. She didn't lose those "stubborn ten pounds" (she liked her body just fine), she capped the alterations at three fittings, and proudly wore the same strapless bra she'd had for years—sagging breasts be damned. Two years after the wedding, their friendship has survived, though I can't say the same for the champagne-colored dress, which police said was rendered beyond recognition.

When you're up against your friend's ridiculous wedding demands, be diplomatic about your role as a bridesmaid. You don't want to let your unwieldy resentment build to the point where your friendship grows toxic, but you don't want to ruin her big day, either. So wear that dress with grace, and take solace in knowing what kind of bride you will be—the laissez-faire kind who lets the girls wear whatever dress they want (except for that one bride who deserves some payback). After all, as bad as that dress might seem now, Halloween is never far away—and you certainly don't have the money to buy a costume this year!

What *Not* to Do as a Bridesmaid

It's one thing to look like a fool (in that dress, it can't be helped), but it's another to *act* like one. With so much pent-up anger and reduced air flow due to the constricting nature of the dress, it's easy to blow your stack. But while you may not have control over the attire, you do have control over your actions. Do not, under any circumstances, no matter how bad the Panic gets, do any of the following:

- Make a really embarrassing sloppy toast that no one will forget.
- Slide-tackle the sweet-as-can-be sixteen-year-old cousin of the bride when she innocently catches the bouquet.
- Get so hammered you puke in front of the minister or shamelessly seduce the teenage catering boy.
- Flip off the photographer . . . and the videographer.

The next time you attend a friend's wedding, reminding yourself to adjust your sour attitude—even a little—in addition to your strapless bra will make the day infinitely more enjoyable. Ignore the moronic comments spewing from people in tacky rental tuxes who can't be taken seriously anyway. Sure, weddings can get us down, but you can't let them sink you! And when all else fails, remind yourself of the debt you're *not* getting into because you didn't spend your last cent on a wedding band aptly named the Vulgar Bulgars.

Remember above all that the bitterness over the one thing you want is the same bitterness that will ultimately impede your hunt for it and what's left of your dwindling mental health. Taking a more sanguine approach, like not pulling the fire alarm during the reception slide show, is the healthiest thing you can do for yourself and your PF search. This is one instance in which you don't want to look younger than you are.

Your friendship with the bride is too important to throw away because of the rocky road to her wedding. You may want to wring her neck now, but it's a real testament to your growth to take the high road and celebrate with her, not sabotage her big day. After all, seeing someone you care about find her beloved should feel like a sweet wine going down, not a concept you're choking on. If a friend just announced her engagement, send her a congratulatory card, not an anonymous death threat. Remember, she will do the same for you one day.

5

How to Project Hotness and Desirability When You Have Neither but Want Both

One of the worst byproducts of the Panic Years is the eruption of self-doubt. Past the age of twenty-five and faced with a coterie of married friends and mounting pressure, even the most self-assured, accomplished woman is a sitting duck for the Panic. Sure, you might be needy in every sense of the word—an SPS starved for affection, companionship, luminescent skin, and two nickels to rub together—but it's these perceived shortcomings that will inevitably cripple your chances of projecting confidence. If you're committed to breaking the panic cycle to attract your perfect guy, you need to get back in touch with the girl whose theme song used to be "I'm Too Sexy," and who made every cad and construction worker alike bay at the moon when she walked by.

PFs smell an SPS's Panic like dogs smell fear. If you're

burying your confidence instead of basking in it, it shows. Obviously each breath you take is a prayer for marriage, but he doesn't need to know that! Projecting self-assuredness and vitality is not just recommended, it's an unequivocal commandment to help conquer the Panic Years. So what if your vitality is as dubious as your "natural nose"? Not to worry: while projecting confidence may not come as easily to you as cellulite does to your thighs, you've seen enough examples of confident women to emulate them convincingly! And if you start by simply acting the part, in time you'll find you've stopped acting and started actually embodying these traits.

The key is to discover how to mask your inner neediness—let them think they need *you*, not the other way around. Here's what you can do to figure out how PFs perceive your panic level, spin a negative persona into a radiantly positive one, and transform your desperation into high desirability.

WHY POSITIVITY BEGETS PFs

During my own time on the singles sidelines, I have never seen an insecure, unconfident bride. I've seen homely brides. I've seen more than my fair share of distasteful brides (baby-pink scalloping . . . c'mon, ladies!). Yet every bride I've seen gracing that aisle has appeared confident, glowing, and happy (even with layers of makeup and inches of hair extensions, you can't fake that). There's no reason we can't project these qualities out into the world in our everyday lives. But more than project it, we must genuinely feel it. Because even the best actresses can't play a role 100 percent of the time.

Most guys (and if you ask them, most women too) are not looking for a pro bono character-building project when they meet someone; they're not looking for a wounded soul in need of emotional resuscitation. Generally, we relate and respond best to upbeat people with an overall sense of positivity and self-worth. If you identify with the statement "It's not that I have low self-esteem, it's just that every guy I pick is better than me," then you just might need an immediate shot of confidence. Remember, people see you as you see yourself, so make sure not to bathe yourself in eau de down-on-your-luck—even though you wear it so well!

The Big No-No: Panic on Parade

Dave is my thirty-year-old friend who could easily fall back on FBI bomb-sniffing work if his career as a pharmaceutical salesman somehow becomes too unstimulating. A more apt name is actually Sniffer Dave, the apropos epithet bestowed on him by all our friends. Like the Smoking Gun has a nose for buried news, Sniffer Dave has a nose for sniffing out singles—and panicked singles at that. He prides himself on being able to detect an SPS's eau de desperation from well across the room.

"I have definitely dated the 'I want to get married' posse," Sniffer Dave says, laughing. He knows that having the Panic is one thing, it's masking it that's half the battle. "It's all these women who were just way too desperate for my taste. It got to a point where I felt that I had to take care of someone, like these women were looking to me to solve all their problems. I want to be in a place where I *want* to take care of someone, someone who can also take care of herself," he continues. "As soon as a girlfriend shows she's needy, any attraction I have toward her instantly plummets." One particular SPS, who was twenty-eight at the time, may have mistakenly tipped her hand with the wrong guy. "She had this plan and was very open about it—get married by thirty, have baby by thirty-two," Dave recalls. "I have a plan too, but as soon as I saw that she had to execute this one, all bets were off." The lesson here? Remember that to rhapsodize the Panic among your trusted friends and family is one thing, to rhapsodize to the world with a bullhorn is another story.

Sniffer Dave terms this panicker purebreed "the Cling-on Girls"—those who, loosely translated, physically attach themselves to a PF, regardless of who he is. "Cling-ons bend in all different directions once they're with a guy. There are no deal breakers. If a guy is within a girl's range—in her ballpark of ideals she's looking for—she will do anything to hold on to him. Then the guy has, like, 80 percent of the power in the relationship." As a rule, most men—the good ones anyway— will marry someone whom they feel is their equal, a partner. Setting your expectations low and letting him wield all the power and run the show because you fear he'll bolt if you do otherwise is a recipe for failure. You'll be used and tossed aside in favor of a girl with a higher opinion of herself.

Moral of the story, ladies: never let 'em see you panic!

Avoid Being Identified in the Panic Lineup

Don't become the punch line of your own panic. There are many measures you can take to mitigate the panic waves you've inadvertently been sending out in high volume. But first, take an honest look in the mirror. Are you screaming "panic" in any of these areas?

Your Dress:

It's the most basic and obvious example, yet so many SPSs make routine fashion faux pas and broadcast their Panic through their attire. Never wear your Panic Years war fatigues around PFs—you want to bring the *right* kind of attention to your body. If you think that going to a party in what look like a stripper's (or Pamela Anderson's) clothes will hook you a PF, think again—that short skirt plus low-cut top equals Panic at its worst! Not only will you not be taken seriously, but you will be automatically classified as someone desperately trying to be noticed—with the *wrong* kind of attention. (You don't want to be the kind of girl who keeps Joan, Melissa, and the rest of the fashion police in business, do you?)

And ODing on makeup screams Panic in the worst of ways. This is a particularly insidious area, since many of us have a terrible blind spot when it comes to our makeup application. Remember, you're not looking to cover up who you are, you're just trying to cover up your outer panic.

Your Attitude:

If you have any sense of proportion left—though considering that an entire box of Krispy Kremes in your apartment disappeared in a day suggests you don't—it's imperative that you avoid being overeager and overanxious in your dealings with PFs. For example: Even though you're thinking, "When can I see you again?" let him be the first to say it. Guys—even the guileless ones—still like to think they're the pursuers, so always let them *think* you need to be wooed, even when you're already won over.

Your Crew:

Traveling in posses of SPSs and standing around anxiously in a panicked-looking cluster, eyes darting at anything that walks

or crawls through the door, is *not* the way to attract your PF.
You are not the *Entourage* crew—this tactic will not translate
favorably for you. Instead, pick one or two of your more confident friends to party hop with you and try to keep an air of
cool indifference.

Your Phone Manner:

Even if you're an innate recluse, when you're on the phone
with a new guy you must force yourself to channel your inner
raconteur. Take heart in knowing that even the most intro-
verted SPS can come out of her shell in this murky medium
of communication.

   Holly, a reformed panicker, used to be a disaster on the
phone with PFs. "I was the most skilled mediator in my office—negotiating conference calls with twenty people—but
when it came to my personal life, I had no idea what I was
doing on the phone!" Finding it difficult to quell her nervousness with guys, Holly would delve into squeamish subjects
like her cat or her grandmother's recent colon surgery, bring-
ing an untimely end to the phone call and the relationship.
She knew she needed to take a more relaxed attitude toward
talking on the phone. "After a while, I realized I needed to
take a new approach on the phone, and decided to consciously keep things much lighter and more fluid. Now, I've
graduated from reading off my prescribed note cards during
phone conversations to 'Holly Unplugged' and I never feel
anxious or agitated on the phone anymore!"

   So whether you relay a funny story about clashing with a
scientologist on the street, mention the Save Darfur rally
(which should earn you humanitarian points), or explain why
you have to get off the phone so you won't miss the addictive
24, the point is to make sure that you sound passionate, positive, and upbeat—and not like some forlorn charity case.

Here's an example of what *not* to do:

PF: Hi! How are you?
YOU: Still breathing, I guess.
PF: Um, I think that's my other line . . .
YOU: Steve? Steve?

Your Topics of Conversation:

Nailing the art of conversation is crucial when you first meet someone, yet it's easy to flub. So you're a doctor working back-to-back overnight shifts with too little time for the gym and too much time for noshing on ever-present hospital rice pudding. While you can dish with friends all you want about how thrilled you are that your scrubs have an elastic waistband, buying you at least an extra three months before anyone notices all the weight you've gained, remember to refrain from exulting too much when talking to a new PF. Women often fall back on self-deprecating humor when they get nervous, but that gaffe projects low self-esteem and is the fastest guarantee that you *won't* be the doctor with whom he wants to set up his next appointment. Remarks such as the following must be avoided at all costs if you don't want your PF to bolt before dessert—or the check—arrives:

- You've just been seated at dinner when you ask if he wants kids, to which he responds, "Um, I think I have a different menu than you do."
- He tells you how nice it is to finally meet you, to which you respond, "Oh, you too! It's been so long since I've been out with someone . . . or out of the house at all. I can't even remember the last time!"

- As he physically sizes you up and you see his eyes doing mental calculations, you assure him, "Yes, these are some serious birthing hips, aren't they?"
- You tell him, "I never want to forget how magical our first date was sixty years from now. Let's promise—right here and now—that we name our first-born after this date; and let's make a pact to name him or her Applebee."

Josh, twenty-seven, recalls an unfortunate date with a panic powerhouse who telegraphed her innermost desires way too soon. On date number two, Chelsea dished about her list of life goals, only it wasn't so much a "list" as it was a single bullet point: "Children, lots and lots of children—all I really want to do is be a mom." On the same date, Josh noticed Chelsea's spoken-for ring finger. When he finally asked what gives, she answered matter-of-factly, "Well, I just couldn't wait anymore! It's kind of embarrassing not to have a ring by this point, and I don't know when I'll have a fiancé to buy it for me, so I just figured I'd save him the trouble down the road and bought it for myself with my bonus from last year!" She assured Josh that when the time came, he shouldn't fret—she would give him the ring so he could propose to her properly. "She actually seemed like a really nice, together person from a distance, but I just wasn't ready to deal with that stuff—much less on a second date!" Josh admits.

Dating with Dignity

Dating with dignity might sound like a contradiction in terms for any SPS in the throes of the Panic Years and accustomed to the all-too-familiar refrain of "Brother, can you spare a date?" But it's not a total impossibility, if you follow these steps. Even the most destitute of SPSs must remember not to emit the scent of despair; pouncing on the poor PF like he's the main attraction at feeding time may be fun at first but all too frequently fails to nail down a long-term commitment. There is a fine line between confidence and desperation. When you approach a guy at a party and say hello, that's not desperation—it's a gutsy and confident overture that would earn any guy's respect. But clinging to his arm all night and waiting until he's tipsy enough not to pass up an invitation back to your place is a no-no. Here are more positive proactive measures you can implement right now to transition from desperate to desirable:

- Wipe off that anxious look you're mugging at parties—keeping a trained eye on the door and scanning everyone who walks in for potential prey—and put on your relaxed one.
- Learn to accept—not minimize—his compliments. When he tells you how gorgeous you look in that skirt, don't point out how it accentuates your hips!
- Go from guarded to gregarious—and watch your stock soar. When you hold back too much and don't open up about yourself even a little, PFs have a hard time convincing themselves to wait until you decide to come out of your well-protected shell, so make sure you let him see your true character while you have the chance.

  Note: Gregarious does NOT mean T.M.I. (Too Much Information!)—ex-boyfriends, financial woes, a body hair issue that just won't quit, or anything else that might depict you as a neurotic downer is off limits at the beginning of a relationship. (Save some of the fun stuff—like that corrected lazy eye story—for later on!)

How One SPS Changed Tactics—And Got Results

It took a few hard lessons before Serena finally learned the difference between masking her desperation and broadcasting it. "I'll never forget the look on my date's face when I made the most embarrassing remark about the melding of our families," Serena, twenty-six, now says, cringing. "When my date told me about his mom's knitting club, I connected that to my own mom's book club, and before I could stop myself, I spontaneously pointed out how well our moms would get along and how much they would have in common when they met!" Serena didn't know guys' eyebrows could raise that high, and her raging overeagerness ensured that these two moms would never be meeting. "Since then, I've been careful not to project so far into the future with a guy I've gone out with one time!"

Ultimately, it's not just projecting confidence that's crucial, it's genuinely embodying it that is. While it's a great feeling to convince PFs of your desirability, it's decidedly more important to convince yourself of it. Just because you find yourself flirting with the Panic Years does not give you latitude to sell yourself short—the common mistake that too many of us make. It might seem impossible now, but you really need to pick yourself up when the panic has you down; feeding on your insecurities only sends the panic to new levels. So remember how much you have to offer and how eligible you are for marriage-minded men. When you truly believe that any PF would be lucky to have you is when you'll see your dating prospects soar.

6

Snap Out of Your Dating Delusions and Start Looking for the *Right* Kind of PF Now

Weeding out guys based on looks and other superficialities might have been something you could get away with back when you were still a knockout, but it's not in your best interest now if you're serious about finding your match. You've got to look a little deeper, both in PFs and yourself, to figure out what kind of person you want, and more importantly, what kind of person you are. The message of this chapter is to be more open to the *right* kinds of PFs—not the fairy-tale notion of them. So toss out the snap judgments and psychological debris you've been storing and be open to finding true and lasting love—without selling yourself short.

When Your "Type" Isn't Really
Your Type at All

A few PFs ago, I was "in love" with someone who I thought embodied everything I wanted in a husband—intelligence, "humanist of the year" pins attached to his lapel, a mutual love for eating summer squash in winter and winter squash during the summer. I was so taken with his external qualities that I convinced myself I was in love with Michael the person, never realizing that I was really in love with Michael the résumé. It was only after our breakup that I realized that the intense feelings I had weren't borne out of anything we generated together, anything authentic—and I really saw him only through the rose-colored haze I had created. My feelings were borne from his list of achievements and surface attributes, which I had admired from afar.

So take heed: projecting your ideal onto your PF isn't the same as him actually living up to that ideal. So he's a masterful concert pianist and composer? Beyond enjoying his music, what does that really do for you? He might be the world's most skilled pilot, but you're not a plane. Those talents don't speak to anything about your relationship or how he treats you or whether or not you'll be happy together fifty years from now. It's what kind of music you make together that really matters. In my case, I created a symphony of self-delusion. I thought I had hit the jackpot with Michael. Only after it was over could I come to appreciate that we had been striking false notes the entire time—but because I was so taken with the *idea* of him and his accomplishments, I didn't even know the difference.

Anyone Who Has a "Type" Also Has a Dating Death Wish

We all think we know our "type," but by virtue of even outlining a type, you seriously risk the possibility of passing over your perfect match. You also might not be ready to digest the prospect of a real, attainable person. The criteria in your mind—physical attributes, career achievements, superficial mutual points of interest—can prevent you from seeing the potential in otherwise eligible PFs who cross your path.

A few PFs ago I dated a steadfast brunette loyalist. "If only you had dark hair," he'd sigh. "I really want my kids to have dark hair." I wondered if he was blind—both literally and metaphorically. Didn't he see my literal true colors at the roots? But that misses the real point by a mile. The truth was that he'd been so fixated on this idea of a perfect brunette counterpart that he wouldn't expand his checklist for anyone who didn't match his mental pre-reqs. We're all guilty of secretly stashing away a certain vision—a working skeletal framework of what we want in a PF—but it's only when we're really ready for love that we bury it for good in the recesses of our minds in the interest of finding something real.

Panickers Can't Be Choosers—or Can They?

Now certainly no one's suggesting that you must cling to the first compulsive gambler who gets down on one broken kneecap and proposes, but in my experience, the lamenting SPSs who apply unrealistic standards to their PFs over and over again are the ones who are still single to this day and consider a vibrating chair the closest thing they have to male companionship.

The Myth of Love at First Sight

How about this unfounded single-girl fallacy? "When I meet my soul mate, I'll know instantly that we're meant to be together." To that, I say, right, keep nursing those wildly unrealistic ideals for another ten years and the appearance of yet another chin. The number of times I've gone on a first date with someone and announced—in my head and thankfully not during the main course—that we'd get married is significantly higher than the number of second dates I actually scored with those same people. It's a nice thought, but the reality is that one "perfect date" does not translate into a perfect life.

Conversely, if you're weeding out prospectives because a first date *fails* to meet all of your ideals, you will forever personify Dali's *El gran masturbador.* Michelle, one especially picky friend of mine, has repeatedly made the claim "I don't want to be with someone who grows on me." She tells tales of woe of dating guys with all the seemingly right moves, but without "the magic." Instead she holds out for that elusive initial chemistry—that feverish excitement rocketing from the pit of your stomach that sends your heart and body quivering to heights you never thought you could experience outside of a bubble bath with Harlequin novel in hand—only to have it fizzle and burn out as fast as a Hollywood courtship. She has crossed over from "refuse to settle" territory clear into the hyperselectiveness highlands—and is paying the costly price for it now, as she's still single at thirty-three and fills in "single and looking" for the marital status question on doctors' forms.

The reasons for her pickiness? "I'm not going to wake up one day and regret marrying someone and get divorced." Okay, but we're talking about giving some guy a second date, not a second kidney. "I'm a very spiritual person—I have a sixth sense, an intuition about people," she insists, "and if the spark's not there on the first date, then it will never be there. If I'm on the first date and I can't envision us having sex, there won't be a second. I'm not going to marry someone just because he's nice."

Now, no one's asking her to marry someone or pretend to enjoy him like A-list celebrities pretend to enjoy courtside seats at Lakers' games when everyone knows they make an appearance solely to milk photo ops. To spin the wheels of someone whose company she doesn't enjoy and whom she merely tolerates would be unfair—but this isn't an all-or-nothing deal. Remember, there's a vast continuum between repulsion and adoration. And as many happily married women will attest, it's very often the guys who surprise you—who start off nondescript but grow more and more charming as you go—who end up being the keepers down the line.

Michelle has endured my relentless counterarguments but has remained resolute about her *unnatural* selection dating routine, refusing second dates to most of the guys who ask for one. Ultimately, very few guys will get a pass based on her unforgiving scoring system. The possibility that attraction builds, especially the enduring kind of attraction—which can be sustained only through heightened emotional and intellectual synergy—isn't even on her mental map. And this certainly isn't helping her tie that knot.

Most WMDs will tell you that the "right" couple doesn't have to harmonize perfectly in the beginning—and in fact most don't. Even the finest musical ensembles must practice doggedly to eventually blend perfectly with each other. You think Sonny and Cher's musical nirvana was achieved overnight? Try nurturing a new relationship and giving it time to develop, and time will tell whether you and your PF are synchronized or not.

Jamie, thirty-one, a newly minted WMD, used to be a Michelle. Things with Sam were plodding along rather than pulsating wildly—until that turnaround moment. That one day when this guy she'd been ho-hum about for two months transformed into someone she couldn't live without. "Things were good, not great, for the first two months that Sam and I were dating. I liked him and he had the qualities I was looking for, but nothing knocked my socks off. He was really nice, just nothing amazing."

One day, though, the feelings and emotions that Jamie didn't even realize she had quickly became self-evident. "He told me he was going away on business for two weeks and suddenly I felt so upset," Jamie recalls of the physical longing she felt because she missed Sam so much. "It was then that I realized how much he meant to me."

Michelle, like many other girls drowning in deep dating waters, is confusing "settling" with building a bond together over time. Remember, it's those same relationships that bristle with the electricity and dynamism that Michelle dreams of that usually fizzle very fast.

Don't Be Fooled by Initial Fireworks

Think of an initially enticing relationship like your favorite food. The first few bites are heaven, as you let the flavors awaken and enliven your senses. The first bite, second, third, fourth—each as satisfying as the last. But by the time you perfunctorily swallow the fifteenth bite, you can't possibly sustain the degree of edifying pleasure you had at the beginning. After the first few bites, the pleasure naturally abates. This kind of situation is paralleled in the early stages of an intense relationship. The first few heady days and weeks and months can taste like heaven, but after some time has passed and you get used to the taste, your enjoyment levels off—and things can become humdrum as hell. When the hormones settle, you may very well find that you and this cosmic counterpart have very little in common except, well, hormones. Jamie's greatest piece of advice: "Just because you don't have *that* on a first date doesn't mean it's not going to work out in the long run. To be honest, I wasn't so sure about Sam in the beginning, but I'm so happy I didn't impulsively end it."

Solid relationships that lead to marriage are usually spared that whirlwind excitement of him not calling for a week after the first date because he was trying out the new "nine-day rule" to see how you'd react. Be honest: that's the kind of "excitement" that most of us can happily live without. So open yourself to the possibility that not lying awake at night fretting over what he's thinking and why he didn't call, not falling head over heels and sleeping with him on date number two, are actually *good* things! Though it's counterintuitive, a calm wait-and-see approach just might mean you're on the right track.

Today, Jamie has a baby and is blissfully in love with the man she's so happy she gave a chance—her adoring husband. And if she hadn't kept giving him chance after chance on date after date, she never would have seen him become the man with whom she has built so many things: a home, love, a family, and perhaps most important, a deck now extending from the kitchen so she can enjoy al fresco breakfasts. "It's a telltale sign of immaturity if you set those ultraspecific parameters," Jamie says. "These women can say they want to get married, but their behavior and actions don't follow suit." It's a lesson to all of us to date more democratically, making sure we don't preemptively dismiss someone for failing to meet the requirements of a checklist we'll most likely throw out the window five years from now anyway.

The greatest gift you can give yourself, if it doesn't come naturally, is forcing yourself to have an open mind; flexibility is your greatest secret weapon in your PF search. Who cares how hot someone is right now if the way he treats you is subpar? You think he'll still look so good later when you see him in such an unflattering light? Five weeks from now, five months, five years, and even fifty years down the line, you'll want to be aligned with someone who shares your interests and values and demonstrates kindnesses, even when no one's looking. The only thing immutable that you can count on is someone's soul; that, unlike wrinkles and waistlines, doesn't budge as long as the person lives.

EX EDUCATION

If you're trying to gauge your feelings for someone new against an ex-PF, you're doing yourself a major dating disservice. By definition, experiencing your *first* love happens, well, only once. If you're worried that the potency won't crest to the same heights with your new PF—you're likely right. But it's not a greater potency that you need, it's an enduring one. Trying to re-create a past relationship is futile and why would you want to? Even if everything was "perfect," obviously there was that one component—maybe the only one, but the essential one—making the difference between it leading to marriage or not. Trying to re-create a relationship that didn't last will only set you up for monumental disappointment.

Focus on What's Really Important Long Term

When my friends are levitating over being "in love" with some new guy, I generally take their mushy musings with a grain of salt—until I get a fuller picture, at least. For instance, my friend Rebecca recently crossed over into questionable waters when I noticed her Friendster profile had changed, and instead of the "single and looking" box, the "in a relationship and just here to help" box was clicked on—the online equivalent of engraved wedding invitations. Now she's here to help? Isn't Rebecca the one who not three weeks ago grabbed the open mike at our friend's wedding and announced to the entire wedding hall that she was available "as a joke"? It's a bold statement—online or otherwise—to change to another box so swiftly.

What is most troubling about Rebecca's new relationship isn't what she says about the guy she's seeing, but what she doesn't say. One red flag is her indiscriminate gushing about everything and nothing in particular: him opening every door for her, taking her to her wish list of plays, saying how incredulous he is that someone like her would date him. Great, so he's preternaturally chivalrous, but when it's just the two of them stripped of external fillers—the big-ticket background—then what do they have? What exactly does she like about him—other than the fact that he really likes her?

She has curiously failed to mention anything about him that's character driven. Yes, I've heard past the point of exhaustion that "he's so rich, even his toilet plunger is classy, and he's soooo sweet," but ask any married person and they'll tell you that "kindness and character" supplant "rich and sweet" every time. Acts of kindness, not just toward you or his inner circle, but toward others, and real evidence of his values and how he lives his life speak much louder than him scoring the theater tickets you've been crowing about.

Listening to Rebecca, I couldn't help but notice that all of her man's admirable qualities seem to relate back to her. He confessed he'd admired her from afar for months but was too afraid to approach this unattainable flower. He thinks she's so beautiful, and so brilliant. Great, that and two dollars gets you on the subway. But what does that do for her besides flatter her ever so momentarily? What about ten minutes from now, when the compliment wears off? Or ten months or ten years from now, when her floral aroma might wear off completely?

Initial dating delirium is not the stuff of which strong foundations are born. It's all too easy to get caught up in a guy who's seemingly smitten with you, but you need to find someone with more sustainable attributes than your mutual love for yourself as the glue to carry you into a long-lasting relationship. Any healthy relationship can withstand some self-scrutiny now and again, so be sure to evaluate your reasons for loving him—without going overboard with your daily checklists—and you'll soon see if yours is made of the kind of stuff that sticks to the wall or not.

Remember, if you find yourself enthusing to friends, "But he has the same Munch *Scream* poster in his apartment!," it's not a sign you're cosmically connected, it's just a sign that your estimation of high art is about as rudimentary as his.

Are They in Bar Mode or Bridal Mode? The Role of Age in Picking a Suitable PF

"No guy should ever get married before he's thirty," my friend Amy, thirty, suggests in a surprising turn of reverse ageism. "They really have to establish who they are first." She asserts that men are providers only by default and that they have to make up lost ground as they mature. In practical terms, this

means you'll want to look for a suitable PF who falls somewhere between the years of graduation from business school
and the graduation to mushy foods in the oldster home.

Amy likes her PFs smack in the middle. "If you're a girl in
your twenties, definitely look for someone older," Amy says
with an authority you don't want to mess with—and the
wedding plans at an upscale Manhattan caterer to back it up.
"Guys want to feel established, like they have the finances to
take care of the girl—and the younger guys just aren't at a
point in their lives where they can do that." That men want
to take care of their women—that they want to be able to
offer them something—is precisely why Amy supports fishing
for a PF in "ancient" waters.

Now, there's no guarantee that a deep-pocketed thirty-
two-year-old who just made partner at his consulting firm
will be any more mature or interested in the concept of marriage than any given twenty-seven-year-old. So keep Amy's
wisdom in the back of your mind while still examining every
PF on an individual basis, with your handy pocket red laser
pointer if needed. Whether a PF is in a serious state of mind
has as much to do with his personal life philosophy as it does
with age. So if a guy detests the idea of being with one
woman at twenty-nine, he most likely won't experience those
elemental feelings at thirty-two or thirty-five either, even
when he is smack in the middle of a marriage.

Lowering the Bar—Are You Digging Too Deep?

When your panic is on the rise, your selectivity can be on the
descent; keep saying everyone's out of your league and you'll
make it happen. If you think he's the best you can do, then he

is. Though it's crucial to establish realistic goals for your PF search, it's still important to retain *some* standards and not lower the bar too much. Here are some scenarios to help you decide whether he's the catch of the day or should be thrown back into the dating pool:

Dating Deal Makers and Deal Breakers for the SPS Savant

You meet him waiting in line for a flu vaccine shot:
DEAL MAKER: He'll be spry all winter long.
DEAL BREAKER: He's eighty-two.

He's in a dodgeball league:
DEAL MAKER: He's athletic, sociable, and has a sense of humor.
DEAL BREAKER: He hurls the ball at your head with the velocity of a speeding rocket.

He excitedly awaits jury duty:
DEAL MAKER: He takes pride in exercising not only his rights as an American, but his responsibilities.
DEAL BREAKER: He says it gives him something to do and he likes the sandwiches they get at lunchtime.

He loves movies:
DEAL MAKER: You share an affinity for avant-garde foreign films.
DEAL BREAKER: He's one of those annoying people who tries to convince you to wait out the extra six months until the public library carries the title for free.

He's sporting a vanity eye patch:

DEAL MAKER: It says, "I'm chic, different, and wildly eccentric."

DEAL BREAKER: It's still an eye patch and you find yourself calling him "matey" without really even knowing what it means.

He's an art enthusiast:

DEAL MAKER: He makes it a point to compliment the pieces around your apartment.

DEAL BREAKER: Last time he was over, he admired a beautiful reproduction, asking if you'd drawn it. You stammer, "You've never seen the *Mona Lisa* before?"

He's a life coach/salsa dancer whose permanent address is his friend's couch:

DEAL MAKER: He's a free thinker who doesn't play by society's rules.

DEAL BREAKER: Um, looks like the life coach needs a life coach. .

He never takes off his baseball cap:

DEAL MAKER: He's an avid sports enthusiast, just like you.

DEAL BREAKER: It screams, "I can't come to grips with my male pattern baldness."

His name is Yale:

DEAL MAKER: Having been taunted from birth until now about his name, he probably has the sensitivity thing going for him. He also comes from a family that clearly values education.

DEAL BREAKER: He cracked in eighth grade when he got a ninety on a math final and wound up in community college, disappointing Yale Sr. and the missus, and now he walks around dejectedly with a "Yuck Fale" T-shirt that reeks of rejection.

Other No-Nos: Where You Have to Draw the Line:

- His method of prescreening you is the ever-discriminating "So, are you an in-network user?"
- His staple story, the nugget you can see he's just bursting to share: his family made two appearances on the *Family Feud* game show (the Louis Anderson version).
- He claims he's Seth Green's half brother.
- He's so painfully boring that his therapist decided to terminate his sessions.
- There's a copy of *Sex for Dummies* conspicuously sitting on his coffee table.
- "I'm off to GA," he announces. "Wow, you have access to the General Assembly?" you ask. "Um, no, Gamblers Anonymous; I've had an addiction since college." "Oh, well that's still cool. Break a leg. Um, if the loan sharks haven't already . . ."

Don't Compromise Your Values, Beliefs, or Ethics in Pursuit of Marriage

Ethics are for suckers, you say? Perhaps. They have no relevance in today's society? Not true on my watch. No PF is worth shelving the steadfast ethics you've upheld for the past few years, or weeks, of your life. Are you selling yourself short—and compromising your principles—in the interest of landing a PF? If politics are important to you and dragging your husband to "Impeach that monkey in the White House" underground meetings is something you've counted on for years, you don't have to sacrifice that component of your character just because an apathetic and apolitical PF is available. There will be plenty of anarchists and liberals out there— there are certainly enough in my section of Manhattan alone—to stockpile for all you politically boisterous SPSs.

Yet, you can't be held prisoner by your unflinching morals all the time either. Moreover, the issues you find important now almost always change over time; finding those perfectly matched commonalities sometimes matters much less down the road than it does now. So be patient and open-minded at the outset; if he's truly the man for you, all his other amazing qualities will soon overshadow any doubts. And as long as he's not asking you to change or suppress part of yourself, there's no reason you can't support each other's life philosophies.

Man-ic Panic: When the Panic Is on the Other Foot

What is Man-ic Panic? Some rare African fungal disease? This malady is much more insidious than anything you can contract from a wild safari. Man-ic Panic is not often talked about and is even less culturally accepted than socks worn under sandals. But the truth is that some guys—possibly lab-created ones—are also guilty of wearing their panic on their sleeve. Sometimes getting married is their raison d'être too.

The bad news: there's no topical cream for Man-ic Panic.

The good news: we're not the only gender that has an inevitable date with the Panic Years! However, you must always be careful around this type of man. Their unbridled eagerness to get married can be deceptively appealing to our single-minded sensibilities, but it's essential to distinguish which men have only generic marriage motives and which ones want you for you.

Melissa, now thirty, gets goose bumps all over her body when she recalls one particularly alarming Man-ic Panic episode a few years back. "This one was definitely a nut," she shudders with less than fond memories from her stroll down Man-ic Panic lane. When her dating stint with a twenty-six-year-old pediatric resident shifted inappropriately to the fast lane—on the second date—she knew this doctor had come down with one serious case of Man-ic Panic. "We'd gone out twice and he was already talking about getting married!" Which probably would have been matrimonial music to any SPS's ears, if only he'd known her last name. "It could have posed a problem drafting the wedding invitations without him knowing some basics, like where I'm from or my last name," Melissa quips. "I genuinely couldn't tell if I had swept him off his feet or he was just that desperate to get married."

So instead of announcing budding wedding plans with this dubious new boyfriend, Melissa invited the desperate doc to her twenty-fourth birthday party so he could meet some counterpart panickers with whom he might find common ground. "I introduced him to my friend Marni, who I thought he'd hit it off with." The following week Melissa came home to a scathing phone message from Marni on her machine: "Hi Melissa, thanks a lot for setting me up with a psycho! All he did was talk about getting married to me!" I think Melissa got her answer.

Jordana, twenty-eight, still shivers when remembering

her Man-ic Panic experience. "This one guy had an agenda
and he was going to execute it," she recalls. "Before we went
out on our first date, he actually asked how I felt about moving to the suburbs, either right away or after the first baby!"
But the prescreening for his future baby bearer didn't stop
there; he wasted no time in asking, "Do you feel comfortable
cooking?" That was when Jordana told him that she was really
just up for a date, not an interview, and right then and there
rebuffed his offer to take her out. "I had to break up with
him," she now laughs. "Before we even really met!" His thinly
veiled agenda was just too much of a turnoff for her to stomach. But that wasn't the last time she crossed paths with what
she had thought to be a rare species. "They are out there. Guy
panickers do exist and are in greater supply than I thought,
even in L.A.!" Jordana's experience proves that feeling trapped
is an equal-opportunity emotion: neither men nor women
like to feel trapped—at least not pre–first date! It's easy to deride these guys as clingy and desperate and, by extension,
overwhelmingly unattractive. But remember, if *we* are this
cold and dismissive toward Manickers, imagine what most
mainstream PFs think about us.

The reason I'm describing these "pathetic, needy losers"
is not just so we can feel a mini pick-me-up jolt—which can
never hurt—but because they are merely us with marginally
more facial hair. These guys, like most other Manickers running loose out there, wanted to leapfrog from a first date to a
serious relationship to marriage by tomorrow. The truth is, no
one wants to date a Manicker—even his female counterpart!

Panic on panic repels, trust me. So hearing that he's itch-
ing to be hitched shouldn't automatically be music to your
ears—he's really PF public enemy number one, and you need
to beware. A good PF doesn't want a desperate significant
other, so why would you want that for yourself? Two panick-

ers whose only mutual goal is marriage don't have enough commonality to build a healthy relationship—and that, more than a killer wedding, is what you really want.

The harsh light I've cast on these outlier PFs is cruel, but necessary in reaffirming your self-worth in your PF search. As warriors on the front lines of the nuptial war, we need to arm ourselves with all the knowledge we need to avoid booby traps that can only remove us further from our ultimate goal and lead to unhappiness down the line.

As you continue on your search for PFs, be as honest with yourself as possible and try to evaluate them with the clarity and wisdom you know you possess. In the past, we've all zigged when we should have zagged, but we can learn from our poor judgment of the past and start looking for a suitable PF now. If your playbook for past relationships hasn't been working, why not get a new playbook and try a new approach? Let's face it: you've grown, you've matured, and you may very well have the early signs of aging to prove it. Doesn't personal growth feel fantastic? Okay, maybe not, but at least you can utilize your dating wisdom by looking for a long-lasting PF, and neither overlooking him for the most tenuous of reasons nor settling for someone who, deep down, isn't the right one for you.

7

Hunting Season:
Where to Find a PF

"I've tried everything!" bemoans Megan, a veteran dater, who's twenty-four. "Speed dating, setups, improv dating!" So what the hell is improv dating, you ask? But hear this: Megan has the right idea. If you genuinely want to push past the Panic Years, you need to entertain the notion of putting yourself out there to cast as wide a net as possible.

Hunting for a PF is both a science and an art. With all the self-congratulatory coworkers, neighbors, and yoga buddies who have that annoying inner glow because they're settled, there is no shortage of "charming stories about how they met" to guide you in your search. In this chapter, you will learn how to forage for the PF of your dreams rather than waiting for him to come to you. You are a marksman, so you need to do your research, and that starts with mining your friends' success stories. Cull how-we-met stories from every WMD you know and then determine how you can translate their tactics for yourself. Keep your eyes open—and rifles loaded—in order to poach PFs in your regular day-to-day activities, as well as notice how many eligible PFs are right under your nose. So they met at some lame corporate law function in Phoenix while sporting those degrading "Hi, my name is . . ." name tags? Start scouting out your own professional opportunities and brushing up on your small-talk skills: "So, how do you like this dry heat?"

Follow these steps and pretty soon you'll be juggling wedding planners *and* taxidermists—who can preserve your PF's head once you've speared him and mounted him on the wall. One thing to remember about your prey: while questionably intelligent, they can discern the difference between a majestic gazelle gliding toward them and a hulking boar stampeding in desperation. Upon contact, always make an attempt to comport yourself like the gazelle—you can devour him like the boar afterward.

The Best Places to Meet a PF

When Sheila, now sixty-one, was twenty-four and smelled the first whiff of the Panic Years, she wanted a doctor. She wanted a doctor real bad. She wasn't sick, at least not physically. But she had a bee in her bonnet for a doctor husband—an idea that still makes this mom of three and grandma of two giggle with a knowing laugh. So she loitered outside the cafeteria of a nearby medical school waiting around for more than the lackluster fish sticks—she was holding out for a much bigger catch. It took only a few feeble attempts at low-level medical chitchat before he surfaced, and a doctor she got (a leading neurologist who might one day be able to isolate an SPS's Panic gene).

Sheila, artlessly unabashed as she may have been, knew what she wanted and went after it—an admirable quality in any sphere. As for you, there's a PF feeding frenzy right under your nose—if you know where to look. And, basically, you should be looking everywhere.

The Workplace

It was the first day of work at one of Chicago's Big Five ad agencies for Beth and Richard—complete strangers at the time—who started orientation on the same day. Both signed the paperwork on their future 401(k)s that, unbeknownst to them, would in time become conjoined 802s. Richard very gallantly guided Beth to the restrooms, hidden on their maze-like floor of cubicles, and even helped her figure out those tricky vending machines. When all the new recruits stormed the cafeteria en masse and socially awkward Richard co-cooned himself at another table, it was Beth who picked up her chin and her tray and befriended the sole loner of the group. By fiscal year's end, Richard had not only devised a clever ad campaign for his biggest client, but devised a phenomenal proposal strategy as well.

While you don't always have to search for someone with your exact professional ideals, people do tend to gravitate toward partners with similar interests, and it can take off some of the initial pressure. In the workplace, where you already spend so much time with a person, you get to see him in many lights—how he responds under pressure and stress, how he communicates, what his rules are on smuggling plum office supplies. It's literally months' worth of trial dating in a very low-pressure environment. Kicking things into high gear is the easy part: when your entire department is out for happy hour celebrating new stock options, you can linger alongside him toward the end of the evening to get some alone time and generate out-of-office romance. If there's one guy you've had your eye on since he single-handedly salvaged your hard drive, arranging for a one-on-one business meeting over dinner to "thank him" is the perfect opportunity for you to showcase your after-work personality.

Volunteer Work

Volunteering is a reward in and of itself. But for Jennifer, who had set up two mutual friends who eventually got married, the reward suddenly became a little sweeter. The married couple suggested that she check out a program at the local community center. While there, she happened upon a bulletin board posting for a volunteer arts and crafts program for sick children. So she went in the spirit of goodwill and there she met Jonathan, her future husband, brightening the lives of some little ones. See, sometimes karma does boomerang in a good way!

　If you feel lost getting started, try narrowing down the possibilities by ruling out volunteer groups that you know might scare off men—like that Libertarian Women for Life group—or ones that conflict with potential sports events, like *Monday Night Football*. And if you can tie in a personal passion—like campaigning for a certain underdog politician—you'll have a very good chance of finding someone who shares your interests.

Panic U.

SPSs can hit the books and graduate from panic at the same time. Like the scores of higher education hopefuls, my twenty-seven-year-old friend Ilyse recently enrolled in a social work master's program and justifies the staggering $34,000 annual tuition as a down payment for the life she's determined to capture with one of the PFs on campus. She has anointed herself program social chair and has proven adept at organizing mixers with the business, law, and med schools. (Come on, do you honestly think SPSs can support themselves on a social worker's salary alone?)

If you're looking to expand your social circle—or perhaps even your mind—going back to school is a great strategy. For instance, MBA programs are ideal because the lopsided male–female ratio definitely works in your favor, and nursing or med school means face time with lots of eligible guys (and their crazy hours mean they'll want to find someone to nest with who's close to home).

"If you play the grad school card, strategize to get into the one with the most eligible single guys," suggests Greg, a recent law school grad, who's engaged to someone he met there. "Most girls I know through law school were definitely there to meet a lawyer. I doubt some of them will practice or even take the bar, because they accomplished what they set out to do on Day 1." And is Greg's future wife one of these girls? "I'm not answering any questions without my lawyer present." Well, at least one person in that relationship will make a great lawyer.

Museums

I once went to a museum. And the story doesn't end there. It was the Van Gogh exhibit at the Metropolitan Museum of Art—tortured, sympathetic, ethos, pathos, logos, the detached ear, the works. Two days later I was walking down the street, kind of bouncing along and having private confabs with myself as I sometimes like to do, when a guy approached me and asked how I'd liked the exhibit. I stared at him for a moment, failing to comprehend, but then he asked, "You were at the Van Gogh, right?"

A museum meeting even led to marriage for the parents of famed publisher Katherine Graham. While her mother was gazing at the gallery exhibit, her father was gazing at his future wife and said, "That's who I want to marry!"

So yes, all the annoying conventional wisdom about museums and art gallery openings can be true. The PF of your dreams just may be languishing there, wasting his life on "art"! Just remember not to camp out at the wrong kind of exhibits: Georgia O'Keeffe, Whistler, or any works with disturbing themes draw exactly the kind of guy you probably want to avoid.

NOT RECOMMENDED: McMARRIAGEABILITY

Nab a nice, hot PF who's surprisingly low in trans fat in thirty seconds or less! They want a visa about as badly as you want a ring. They need a one-way ticket out of former Communist countries and you need a ticket out of the singles' table. Your U.S. status: an SPS's new currency? We've all seen the Web postings from a rainbow coalition of foreigners searching for citizenship . . . and a wife. Why not consolidate two tedious processes into one? "I am student in Rwanda and want to find a girl to marry and get nationality of USA and settle there forever." This one sounds like a war-torn winner!

Let's examine the facts: they seem to want to settle down, they probably pack light, they must have great stories about revolutionaries and de facto dictatorships, and all they want in return is the latest info on Brangelina and a warm body to sleep next to at night. But you're treading into dangerous territory here—even if you ignore those two hundred motivated Mexicans on bended knees in favor of that cute Aussie guy at the bar who seems legit. The bottom line is, can you ever really know if they're interested in you or your green card? Foreigners looking for citizenship are a unique form of Manickers and have been known to jump ship as soon as the ink on the paperwork is dry.

The Trusted Standby: Singles' Events

Sure, just the very term "singles' event" can make anyone cringe and run for the hills, but today's events are organized in such a low-key way that there's no reason to wear a paper bag over your head at these things. These ain't your mother's sock hops!

Speed dating, for example, may have been the butt of many a joke in the past, but it's completely accepted now—and, given the right setting, really fun. If you're the kind of girl whose schedule generally permits her to meet twenty guys in a solstice, now you can meet twenty guys in an hour! Even if half of them are so unsavory they make Marilyn Manson seem clean-cut, that still leaves actual face time with a good number of real prospects who are clearly motivated to meet someone. They say you shave seven minutes off your life

with every cigarette, and most of these PFs have fewer car-
cinogens than your average Camel, anyway, so what's the
harm in talking for seven minutes? You never know if he
might say just the right thing to make you melt in that time.

If you prefer a mellow scene, singles' wine-tasting events
are offered on an ongoing basis and provide a fantastic backdrop for kick-starting conversations. In her panic prime, an
SPS can feel like a too-ripe wine—but that doesn't mean you
shouldn't check out this fruitful scene where guys are bound
to have a level of sophistication beyond Coors Light. Selecting
the perfect PF is like selecting the perfect wine, maybe even
harder. Just remember—when a PF describes himself as "complex, very ripe, rich, and yeasty," he may be cheesy for ripping
off the label of a cheap Cabernet, but as long as he doesn't
boast about "lacking in acidity and depth," keep an open
mind. After all, there's no excuse to drink alone at these things.
So grab a good friend and treat yourself to a nice bottle.

Setups

You might have thought you were above setups in the past,
but that was before your panic was like an out-of-control
freight train: are you going to let it crush you or do you have
the common sense to run to safety? Forget whatever stigma
you think is associated with this time-honored tradition because setups yield high returns on the PF front.

Yes, for the uninitiated, these dealings can border on the
embarrassing. But once you get past the initial stiff ice-
breakers ("So, _____ tells me you're a _____ . . ."), there's
no reason why the rest of the date shouldn't be smooth sail-
ing. And in this information age, you can ascertain data like
birth records, bank statements, and his college GPA to ease

your mind before meeting him (and officially make yourself an FBI security priority).

Asking friends, coworkers, and anyone else you haven't offended too much to think of a PF prospect for you is the smartest move you can make. In order to reach liftoff with your love life, you must take the initiative boldly, not sheepishly with down-turned, embarrassed eyes. Confront your friends about fixing you up; they should be more than happy to brainstorm for guys, and seeing you get out of the house on a Saturday night is reward enough for them! You might *think* you know all of your friends' friends, but there's always someone new to the social circle or newly single. And remember, even if it seems like the pickings are slim, it's not important that they know seventeen available men—they just need to know one nice one!

Find the E-Love

Stigma is a thing of the past for digital dating! An entire medium cannot bear all the blame for the distasteful drones roaming about. After all, there are surely freaks zipping through the bar circuit too. Even if you were once guilty of thinking, "I'm twenty-two. I'm too young to do Internet dating. I'll wait 'til I'm twenty-four and desperate," you needn't feel embarrassed about exploring this wildly successful medium now. Not quite as reliable as meeting through a trusted friend, but less embarrassing than a poetry slam, e-dating doesn't carry the shame it once did. The great thing about Internet dating is that it allows you to shop for PFs when and how you want—on the couch, in your sweats, or while on the phone with a friend—no one on the other side of the screen will ever know! And for women whose eighty-hour work weeks preclude any chance of meeting someone in the outside world, it's a technological blessing for your dating life.

More than a few SPSs have admitted they're too proud to dabble in digital dating. And to that I say, "When the hell have 'SPS' and 'proud' ever been in the same sentence?" In the interest of exploring all of your available resources, you must give everyone—and every medium—a fair shot. These waters are too good not to surf in them.

Nikki, twenty-nine, admits she owes her recent engagement to Jonathan to the Internet—and I guess, by extension, to Al Gore. "If Internet dating didn't exist, I would have felt helpless; I was finished with leaving things to chance or fate." Skeptical about online dating after ending a seven-year relationship, she tested the waters by gently dipping her toe into the online dating pool. "I was overwhelmed and unimpressed at first," she said, recalling the avalanche of questionable on-liners who initially contacted her. It took several months of weeding through "the weirdos and the cheeseballs" before one particular snowflake melted her heart. "At first, I wasn't even going to give Jonathan a chance when I saw that he was divorced," Nikki admits, "but we had so much in common that I figured I had nothing to lose." Today, she's certainly grateful that she got beyond her online hangups. Take your cue from her, and fire up that hard drive.

Colorful Online "Personalities": Look Over or Pass Over?

You're a Doctor, We Get It

His screen name is Dr. Awesome. Okay, so creative he's not, but he is a doctor and he is apparently awesome, so don't rule him out just yet. Your instinct might be to delete this guy, but take a deeper look inside. His profile reads: "Hi there, I'm a doctor. While not at the hospital, I enjoy not only boxing, but kickboxing as well. Did I mention I'm a doctor??" And his pictures—shockingly—reveal him wearing scrubs and standing in front of one of those creepy skeletons. This MO also applies to investment bankers, hedge fund managers, rock stars, guys with Pulitzer Prize awards prominently displayed on the back mantle, or anyone else trying a little too hard to capitalize on the allure of their profession (or their paycheck).

To delete or not to delete?

Okay, so this one's swatting at a fly with a jackhammer, but surely you can make allowances for overeager PFs trying a little too hard to compose a perfect package to send to the online world. Give him a chance, don't give him the boot!

The Online Apologist

His profile reads: "I can't believe I'm on here, but due to my nonstandard schedule, I've had to resort to online dating . . ." The rest of this prospect's fumbling explanation doesn't really help his cause here. Sounds like he's trying to legitimize his presence on the site to himself more than to potential dates—thereby demeaning the women who are on the site too. Like you, obviously.

To delete or not to delete?

Anyone so embarrassed and clearly uncomfortable with himself that he brings *more* attention to the fact that he's partaking of online dating has too many personal issues that are likely to manifest themselves in various ways throughout a relationship. This one needs to go with one swift click of the delete button.

I Aced My SATs

If his stellar academic achievements of 1993 are making their way into the exclamation point portion of his dating profile of today, you should automatically deduct one hundred points from his online score. With a winning opener like "When I moved to this country from Ukraine and didn't speak a drop of English, I took the SATs and still got into a top Ivy League college," it's like wading through a swamp to even get to the "I am an avid ornithologist in my downtime" comparative profile highlight.

To delete or not to delete?

This charmer of a canary likely sings his own praises too much to ever appreciate a bird of another feather. I have a twenty-five-cent SAT word that he might have to get used to: solitude.

How to Get Past Your Own Snap Judgments

Sometimes the facade haplessly tacked onto PFs' profiles misrepresents them, so it's essential that you try to look beyond the cosmetics and give online PFs the benefit of the doubt. It's all too easy to see flaws while shopping online—and those hi-res photos aren't helping anyone's case. Most online daters are guilty of hastily dismissing a prospect for the most insignificant of reasons. We tend to be much pickier online than in person; if merely one prism of his personality is perceived as "off-putting," we'll immediately click to the next PF. In person, we're much less harsh. I mean, you can't just click a delete button in someone's face—that would be poor form.

So don't let your online hangups hinder your chance at

romantic happiness. While it's true that you can't glean from someone's online profile that his laugh—and financial portfolio—will sound like music to your ears, you'll have ample opportunity to find this out for yourself—if you give him a chance! Online shopping is a mere entrée into someone's personality, the rising of the curtain to a PF's story—but it's a start. So allow yourself to correspond with the sweet guy who sends an e-mail message your way, even if he doesn't fit the paradigm of a hottie PF you initially envisioned. You just might be pleasantly surprised.

The Gym Burns Off the Fat *and* the Panic

Cultivate a more desirable body and a relationship with a PF at the same time! You spend enough time ensuring your physical health at the gym, so you might as well use the time to your full advantage! Cute gym attire and flushed and rosy cheeks can work to distract any PF from that annoyingly perky personal trainer. Even if you think you can bench-press that peaceful-looking PF over in the meditation room, he just might be an ideal candidate.

Pros and cons of intra-gym dating:

Pluses: He's already seen you in some unflattering poses, not to mention heard those unseemly noises you're emitting—grunts only a mother could love. And he's still interested. This one's a keeper!

Minuses: He started crying when the five-pound supplemental weight ruined his new manicure.

While jazzercise with the elderly and unemployed set smack in the middle of the day might be more your speed, it's not going to give you face time with the PFs who regularly attend spinning classes at night. So choose your times and your wardrobe wisely. If the idea of meeting someone without makeup has you ill at ease, try a makeup line tailored to women who work out and start boosting enough confidence to break the ice with someone!

So whom should you approach? The guy prominently sporting that Duke Law T-shirt—he's practically screaming, "I'm looking for a wife!"—is the perfect candidate to sidle up to at the next spinning class or when he's hitting the juice bar. Initiating a conversation can be as casual as coyly asking for his help adjusting a stubborn machine or making a remark about his shirt. Or if you notice him reading the *Economist* on the treadmill sans iPod, don't miss the perfect opportunity to flex your cerebral muscles with your know-how about the European markets.

Ultimately, the gym can be the ideal place to find someone who enjoys the same activities you do: fitness, or at least preening in front of the mirrors long enough to make sure they're working just fine. As a bonus, this ideal PF-hunting site will help you sculpt your body—an important asset in your search.

Remember: forcing yourself to look beyond your current PF purview can make your Panic a hobby of the past. If you earnestly hit the PF pavement with a little ingenuity and an open mind, your previously crippled search can become a hugely constructive one. You needn't be on digging duty 24/7—fifteen-minute catnaps are, of course, allowed if not encouraged—but keeping a regular eye out for a PF is always a good idea when it comes to putting yourself on the marital fast track.

8

Keep Your Friends Close and Your Single Friends Closer

It takes one to know one. Any SPS can sniff out her fellow panickers as fast as she can spot a cubic zirconia stuffed inside a fake Tiffany's box. If your panicked friend has no imminent chance of getting married—and the only prospect on the horizon is her dentist's nephew who's supposedly getting out of a relationship—then she doesn't want you jumping the line to matrimony either. Steadfast fellow soldiers trapped in the foxhole together, you're not. If anything, she's more likely doing espionage for the other side—her own.

This chapter will show you how to distinguish true friends from the toxic ones, monitor your own levels of friend contempt, and repair a ruptured relationship with a WMD. It will also show you how to be strategic in your socializing— because hitting a party with a posse of fellow panickers is the fastest way to send eligible guys running in the opposite direction.

Hitting the Town with a Fellow SPS Means Double Trouble

So it's girls' night out—just you, Tara, Cara, Dara, Mara, and her out-of-town cousin, Farrah. You're all clutched arm in arm, like one big Panic Years chain comprised of needy, codependent links. Trouble's a-brewin', though. Tara is secretly peeved with Dara for stealing the attention of her best guy friend from college, Glen. Glen's friend Len harbored a crush on Mara, but Cara told Ken that *she's* secretly in love with Len. This tattered posse has more thorns than a briar patch. Be mindful: five girls, albeit all desperate, and five guys does not automatically translate into five marital miracles.

If you think your chances of meeting a PF multiply with each SPS who joins your fishing expedition, think again. Running to the bathroom to sort out who gets who is a recipe for broken friendships: "Well, he went to the same fat camp as my sister, so I think I'm entitled to him." You'd be amazed at how many well-adjusted women bring out the claws when panic and a cute, available guy collide on the dance floor.

It's understandable that our eyes start to narrow and fists clench when merely thinking about a fellow panicked friend. "If they're still single," you think, "what does that say about me and my chances of meeting someone?" Or, when a fellow SPS seems to have met someone with potential, we find ourselves seething, "Why not me?" The real-life ramifications of the Panic Years don't just affect you, they affect everyone in your orbit—and often take a toll on your other relationships. The Panic manifests itself in the ugliest of ways and turning on one another is just another symptom.

When this symptom of the Panic seeps in, it usually starts with subtle changes in your friendships. Who does Erica think she's fooling when she swears that your hair doesn't look frizzy? There's no way after that rainstorm that you wouldn't pass for Einstein's finger-in-a-socket-loving descendant. So she'd rather see you get struck down by lightning than see you with a guy. The key here is not to take it personally—an element of competition is inevitable. Is it a coincidence that in her drunken venting sessions she bellows, "If another one of my friends gets married before me, I'm going to shoot myself!"? So keep your cool and let the fact that she finds you threatening become a confidence booster.

If you are on a genuine marriage mission, grab a good guy friend—homosexuality optional—or a cute married friend who knows how to work a room and who will be understanding enough to scoot when you hone in on that "someone special." Having to attend to female friends even needier than yourself while looking for your long-term love drains far too much of your energy. Knowing that they even require accompaniment to the self-help section of the bookstore should have tipped you off that they're not party material.

Types of Toxic Friends

Often we've been friends with someone for so long that we initially overlook the downslide into panic. They're your friends, so clearly you enjoy their company and support, but suddenly they're doing you more harm than good. In the following example, see if you can differentiate the true friend from the toxic one:

> **YOU:** "Great news, guys—Alan just invited me to fly home with him to Chicago to meet his parents!"
> **STEPHANIE:** Hugs you and tells you how great she thinks it is that you and Alan are getting serious.
> **TYRA:** Has a distressed look of concern with the deepening forehead ridges to prove it, as she derides Alan as cheap for failing to pay for your ticket to *his* hometown.

The bottom line: Like these two night-and-day responses, friends' panicked personas can be quite glaring and easy to spot. If the Tyra in your life has been experiencing similar fine-line problems every time you mention your love life, it's time to acknowledge that you have a toxic friend in your midst and proceed with caution. Here are some of the typical toxic types to watch out for:

The SPS Saboteur: If She Can't Have Him, Neither Will You

Lois, forty-eight, is happily married. As if that isn't bad enough, she's trying to spread the blinding sunshine of marital bliss in hopes that the twenty-something set can extract some light from it. But when she got married twenty-five years ago, her best friend of fifteen years peeled off her mask to unveil an out-and-out bitch beneath the surface. Unbeknownst to Lois, her best friend was an SPS saboteur.

"Arlene and I used to travel together and go out all the time. We'd been inseparable since we were ten years old," Lois recalls. But ten turns into eighteen, and eighteen into twenty-two, when, in those days, if you weren't shacked up by college graduation, you were screwed. "Arlene was teaching with my now-husband, Mitch, but she fixed me up with another teacher, one I think she knew I wouldn't like. He was bald and pretty heavy. He was in Mitch's department and she told him about me and he pressed Arlene for my number. He was a nice guy, so when it was obvious on the date that it wasn't working out, he actually suggested I go out with Mitch." Shortly after, Lois asked Arlene about getting set up with Mitch, only to have Arlene immediately dismiss the idea.

"Arlene harangued for a while about how I'd be wasting my time with Mitch, how he wouldn't be right for me," Lois recalls. But she demanded his number and after much haggling, she and Mitch finally found their way to each other. The rest is history. Except for Lois and Arlene's friendship. The two women remained friends, but more than a modicum of trust was lost in the process. "I don't think she was crazy about the idea of losing her traveling mate and her friend to go out with, which is understandable," Lois reasons, "but I have to say that I think our friendship would be stronger now had she been more supportive of my relationship with Mitch. But you never know—I might have felt the same if the tables were turned."

Can You Get Past the Panic?

If a panicked friend deliberately tries to wrong you—or tries to keep you single longer than she is—it might not be so easy to forgive and forget. When trust is fractured that badly in a friendship, the residual sting doesn't dissipate fast and you might be better off ending the friendship—or at least taking a break. But then again, if Paris can forgive Nicole (and Lois can forgive Arlene), then there's hope for the rest of us too.

The Opportunist: She Wants to Be Friends with Your Rolodex, Not with You

Friendships are always cyclical. You may have childhood friends who've fallen off the map, college friends who've fallen off the wagon, and new friends made in early adulthood who end up being the lifelong ones you'll treasure like the semiprecious gem of a friend they really are. Usually, these cycles of friendship are perfectly natural. But beware: sometimes friends can become user SPSs. There are certain telltale signs to watch for.

At a party a few years ago, I introduced myself to a friend-of-a-friend who barely managed to wait the requisite fifteen seconds so it wouldn't look tacky before she asked, "Are you single?" and then launched into the next question: "Do you know any cute single guys?" It was like watching a very efficient wizard brandish his wand. I nodded, befuddled, at which point she wasted not a moment to endear herself to me. "You do? Really? We should definitely be friends!" she emphatically singsonged. Whew! So glad I have something besides my biting acerbic wit and sensitivity to bring to the friendship table; I bring something more elusive—single guys!

She told me that she'd made a promise to herself to get married by her twenty-sixth birthday. Turns out she did. Not that I know much about her life now. Because sure enough, she dropped me like a stick of dynamite once she got a serious PF.

Can You Get Past the Panic?

Is this really what true friendship is all about: caring, compassion, and providing a thick Rolodex of single men? Be warned: in the Panic Years, when new females glom onto you for your friendship, it's probably not for your bubbly wit and personality as much as it is for your party invites, putting your newfound friendship into a clearer context.

This kind of friendship may have its uses but is destined to have an abbreviated shelf life: an SPS has no time for meeting new friends just for the pleasure of their so-called company. In the end, this is the kind of friend you can easily do without. While it's always a great idea to try to expand your social circle, just make sure you do so with people whose self-motivated interests aren't so thinly veiled.

The Zapper: She Who Zaps What Little Life Is Left in You

There are just certain unfailing truths in life: you will never be too thin to donate blood, you sound even more déclassé when you try to speak French—and more so when you say "Pardon my French"—and certain people are simply zappers: those who zap away what optimism, confidence, and energy you have left inside you. They more than taint the room, they taint your very outlook—possibly irreversibly.

After a disappointing night out on the town, one of my SPS friends looked at me over her chipped mug of coffee and dejectedly declared, "It looks like our generation of women just isn't going to marry." After which I excused myself to use the bathroom, hoisted myself through the window, and never looked back. All I asked for was a shot of hazelnut in my coffee, not a treatise from a nut trapped in a negative haze.

What's the only thing worse than unabated cheerfulness from a perennial Pollyanna (i.e., the panicked friend who emphatically slurs, "This is soooo our year!" when she pecks you perfunctorily on the cheek on New Year's)? Unabated sourness. And endless lamenting over bad dates, disappointing men, and the sad state of twenty-first-century romance. If you have encountered any friends that fit that description, make sure you've fashioned an escape route before the sourness really goes rotten.

Can You Get Past the Panic?

If you have become friends with one or more zappers, or a formerly good friend has suddenly become one, use your trusty "sweatpant couture" ensemble that you knew would come in handy some day and run for your life. The quickest way to shatter your already shaky morale is to surround yourself with negative SPSs. If you think your own negativity permeates a room, imagine your friends three years older—three more years' worth of bad dates, three more years of wild-card PFs, all culminating in what's known as Compound Panic Years. It's practically airborne and you don't want to find yourself in the grip of their panic as well as your own. This is one instance in which I pause to celebrate my favorite mantra, "Don't spread the hate!" When it comes to panic, it should always be self-contained.

The logic behind Compound Panic Years is simple: their panic begets more panic. So when they moan in misery to you about being single, be strong and do not let them spread their canopy of contempt over you! Negativity is infectious! Even if you've never smoked a cigarette in your life, you can walk into a roomful of smoke and emerge a smoker. So leave them to stew in their own cauldron of contempt; she's going to bring down your mood and your chances of finding someone right along with her if you don't get out of this destructive friendship.

"IN A FRIENDSHIP, THERE'S ONLY ROOM FOR ONE SPS": PHYSICS FOR PANICKERS

More pernicious than a so-called friend getting engaged is the one who's as single as you are. Sir Isaac Newton once decreed that by the laws of physics, no two panickers could or should be friends, for their safety and the safety of any man who should cross their path, as evidenced by the following formula:

$$\frac{SPS}{SPS} = ca \text{ (combustion) (acceleration)}$$

It's the lesser-known corollary of Newton's Law of Commotion. If he thought the panic was elevated in the seventeenth century, he'd surely roll over on his Bunsen burner if he saw what progress we've made in heightening the panic over the centuries.

CAN TWO SPSs EVER SURVIVE ONE FRIENDSHIP?
If you promise not to let the Panic contaminate your interactions—or if you become a lesbian—then yes, there's no reason why your friendship and all your limbs can't stay intact.

Are You Becoming Toxic Yourself?

Anybody can sympathise with the sufferings of a friend, but it requires a very fine nature to sympathise with a friend's success.

—*Oscar Wilde*

Every seven seconds in this country, some undeserving bitch gets a proposal—a statistic more grim than national high school dropout rates and worldwide inadequate health care realities combined. I came into the line of fire of one such proposal recently when I was out with my friend Julia one evening. We stopped dead in our tracks when The Call came. For all our cutting-edge technology—medical advances, technological discoveries, scientific breakthroughs—can't some research dweeb who took his sister to the prom come up with a special ring to detect the news of *another friend getting engaged*?!?! This time, after answering, my friend Julia made no attempt to feign excitement as she had with the last five of her friends' engagements. You could actually hear her heart sink. It was at this moment that she needed to fight with all her strength to avoid the negative spiral of "it's just not fair" despair that we'd witnessed in so many other friends gone toxic.

Even for those of us with stalwart minds and hearts, it's a fine line between chastising your toxic friend and becoming one yourself. Here are some warning signs that you're testing higher in levels of friend toxicity:

1. You've Invented Panic-ese—A Language All Your Own

You've created an entirely new lexicon for the singles tribe to converse in.

Bitter single's message:	Panic-ese translation:
"Oh, your engagement ring is so delicate!"	"I didn't realize these things still come in cereal boxes . . ."
"I'm sure you guys will really grow in your love over time."	"I'm sure you two will learn to fake mutual affection in time."

"Don't you look gorgeous!"	"I'm not trying to be unkind, but I've seen beached whales more attractive in a wedding gown."
"What a killer dress! Where did you get it?"	"Fire sale at David's Bridal?"

2. Your Friends Fear "Breaking the Bad News" to You

My newly engaged friend Kelly spent a week agonizing about "breaking the bad news" to our mutual SPS friend. "The one call I was dreading was the one to Lauren, who I was too afraid to tell I got engaged. She'd been having a really hard time lately and I thought this news might send her over the edge," Kelly confided to me, in a tone of almost genuine concern. So I personally undertook the onus of sitting down with Lauren to cushion the news. Her response was the expected "It's so hard. How can I be happy for someone else?!" plaintive single-girl psalm. And I guess that was the answer; she couldn't, and was therefore perilously close to crossing over into toxic water.

"The hardest part of all of this is facing the music with my friends," said Shari, twenty-seven, who recently became engaged. "My friends always play the game 'Who's Next?'— when those of us with serious boyfriends announce a trip, everyone speculates excitedly, 'Who's neeeext?' " Until it was Shari who was next and she was met with disappointment and resentment from her closest crop of friends. The problem was she hadn't "waited her turn." "They think I jumped the line," an exasperated Shari told me. "I guess technically I wasn't next, having dated Scott for only a year, but I didn't re-

alize how much that would anger everyone." Even among the
happily dating, the race is always on.

Shari thought her friend Allison, who technically had
been next in line, had recovered from the blow until she got
an ominous phone call. It was Allison's boyfriend. "He called,
frantic," Shari told me. "He said he didn't know what to do,
that she'd been crying for two weeks straight, thinking she'd
be in my wake." Allison was afraid that the tidal wave of
Shari's relationship would drown out the pleasant ripples of
her own and internalized it, like all jealous friends tend to do.
But Shari was doing her best to handle the awkward situation—that is, until Allison's mother brazenly called Shari.
"Her mom called me, crying that Allison was just devastated.
She asked me to help, but I didn't know what to do. I was annoyed that my friend couldn't be happy for me!"

And then "nervy" jumped to "one hell of a lot of nerve."

"Allison's mom then asked me—and I don't know how
she did it with a straight face, 'Can you just check with her
about your flowers and color scheme? She's afraid that your
wedding is going to upstage hers.' I had to consult my friend
about a 'color conflict' and she wasn't even engaged yet?!"
Shari recalls with rightful disbelief. But she was a real soldier—and in the end deferred to the imperious lieutenant Allison. She thought, after all, chocolate and pink color schemes
are temporal; nut job friends like Allison are forever.

How to Temper Your Own Toxicity

It's all too easy to turn on your friends—especially when it
seems like they have the world on a string and all you have are
large pores. But to rupture a friendship, and to bring yourself

down in the process, is no way for a self-confident woman on the road to conquering the Panic Years to act. Don't let your bitterness boil over, burning every friendship you have. No self-assured, positive person should have friends who feel the need to wear kid gloves around her. You don't want to become some one-woman force of nature whose ill will toward her friends spirals out of control, do you? Good friends are one of the key components to surviving the Panic Years—so attract good friends by being one yourself.

The Other Side of the Singles' Aisle: Sanctimonious and Engaged

For all the WMDs who feel slighted by their begrudging single friends, there's the flipside experience of the haughtily nuptialed who can't wait to rub it in. Why don't they just save everyone time and energy and brandish that much-vaunted rock where it really belongs: on the *middle* finger. That's what I'll do when I get engaged, because really, that's what they're all saying to the rest of us. "Fuck you, singles. We did it! Ha!" Brandishing that badge of honor is all the validation this breed will ever need.

My newly engaged "friend" who of course was infinitely more likable before she got engaged now wildly gesticulates with the paw I've barely seen her budge in the ten years I've known her. All of a sudden, she must draw my attention to her ring finger, like she's practicing Klingon out of nowhere—practically shouting "Get a good look!" from her bullhorn. For the panicked SPS, the one friend who's more demoralizing than the moaning single sister is the one who's newly engaged and proud of it. While some women handle this transition with grace, others brandish their victory in the most vulgar way possible.

Last spring I ran into my quasi-friend Kate, whose engagement I got wind of through her mass "GOOD NEWS!!!" e-mail that was so damn singsongy it could have made you puke. When I saw her for the first time in person post-engagement, the first words fired out of her mouth weren't "I'm so happy I met the love of my life!" or even "I'm so happy that I'm finally financially set for the rest of my life!" but instead, "So how's Jennie doing? Still at the same job? Still not dating anyone? Still miserable?" referring to one of our more panic-prone friends.

It was then that it occurred to me: some people don't get engaged for engagement's sake, they do it to spite their single friends. I'd always had my doubts as to whether Kate really had any feelings for that smarmy stockbroker and now her petty post-engaged behavior really put an X-ray up to the darkest cavities of her soul. But how else would someone like Kate derive true happiness? Certainly not from her fiancé, even though she'd told me repeatedly that he's made a killing in the East Asian markets. Nope, it's sticking it to the single girl—the ultimate news guaranteed to silence her forever.

WMD SOAPBOX SUPERIORITY—
THE WORST OFFENDERS:

- "We're going to find you a husband tonight!"
- "I just got my wedding dress. It is soooo gorgeous! Actually, it would look really good on you; I can pass it on to you after, if it's still in style by then."

- "You're never going to get married if you stay in New York. Girls never get married there! Move somewhere else—anywhere!"
- "Jonathan just got us matching husband–wife bracelets for our three-month anniversary—isn't that amazing?!"
- You run into a high school friend you haven't seen since graduation ten years ago. She gives you her trademark hollow hug and asks, "Oh, you're still single?" with her equally trademark insincere concern. "Oh, that's so sad . . ."

But don't worry, there's a special place in hell for these people. Ironically, it's now Kate who's been indignantly silenced, after her fiancé called off the wedding a month before showtime. Oh, and coincidentally, Jennie has never had so much spring in her step.

Just because a friend has graduated from the Panic Years and you still might be on high honor roll doesn't mean the tide of your relationship has to turn to choppy waters. It may take some time before you both acclimate to your new roles, but the presence of a new PF shouldn't make an otherwise close friendship feel altogether foreign. Remember all the wonderful moments you shared before she upped and got herself a hearty meal ticket named Stu, and cut her some slack during the wedding planning phase. Try to suggest any social activity that doesn't involve dress shopping. There is room for peaceful coexistence if you're both willing to work at it.

Moral of the story: don't let the Panic taint your friendships, either with fellow SPSs or WMDs. Be smart about who you choose to surround yourself with, and if they have less than unimpeachable motives, know when to walk away.

9

The One Who Got Away

I'm guilty of a few transgressions that are against my better judgment: due to my blessedly luminescent skin, I got away with student discounts at Kohl's without even having to flash my expired student ID card for years. When my neighbor was away on vacation, or in the shower, I would smuggle his *New York Times* and read it before he even noticed it was missing. And on Sundays, I used to have the devil's ink tattooed across my body, tipping more than just my hand—tipping the scales of my very mental balance.

This devil's ink of which I speak wasn't just a superficial imprint on my skin, it was a needling mark on my very soul. It was the newsprint from the *New York Times* wedding announcement section, and yes, the wedding sections of every major newspaper in the tri-state area. It contributed to Sunday routinely devolving into a macaroni-and-cheese-inhaling torture session, thanks to the cruel insistence by the power-tripping *Times*'s Sunday Styles editors on printing "happy" stories about "young" couples. For my safety and the safety of others, I was forced to cancel my subscription to the paper and child-block myself from the *Times*'s Web site. Thus, pilfering the paper from my neighbor's doorstep had become my only real option.

Wedding announcements: the literary stun gun to an SPS's joie de vivre, or motivation for the PF search? In this chapter, we'll take a closer look at why wedding announcements can make a grown panicker weep; how to stop the cycle of self-destructive behavior that keeps you from moving on; how you can use wedding announcements to your advantage; and how to get past the PF who's gotten over you . . . and gotten engaged.

Don't Surrender Your Sanity to the Wedding Announcements Section

"Sometimes, I can't believe I made the Times."
—*Anonymous annoying WMD*

"Is there a reason to get married other than to be in the Times*?"*
—*same anonymous annoying WMD, as an afterthought*

All wedding announcement sections—whether they appear in your local paper or your high school alumnal magazine—can really drive an SPS to madness. But the worst of the lot is the *New York Times* Sunday Styles section, in which dozens of privileged and complacent twosomes nationwide showboat to millions of readers each and every tedious detail of their lives and wedding. The only real purpose of appearing in the esteemed Sunday Styles section is to convey your status—wedded and otherwise—to the masses. For the SPS, this infamous section evokes and unlocks a mishmash of raw emotions—scorn, rage, hope, and wrath, all while you're loving/hating every minute of it. This may seem incongruous, but it was both the bane of my existence and also my single reason for getting out of bed on Sunday mornings. It's just like a celebrity starlet's public gaffe—you can't look away.

The Worst Wedding Section Offenders

Baby Brides

Have you ever had one of those days? The ones so dismal that you think you'll never summon the strength to crawl out of your cave of despair? Who hasn't? More often than not, it's precipitated by what starts as a casual perusal of the wedding section. And what it often becomes is you demanding aloud and quite thunderously, "What is it? Neo-nuptial day?" Young you can handle—maybe twenty-seven and litigating unhappily at a top five law firm—but this, this is too much. Twenty-two-year-olds who presumably met over their own piles of poop in nursery school! These charmless backstories are way too offensive to be cute, leaving you to wonder why there are such a disproportionate number of trust-funded twenty-two-year-olds named Windsor getting married anyway.

Of course the only blanket of solace in which a panicker can wrap herself is the knowledge that by the time their divorce rolls around, when they are in their late twenties, they'll still have all that baby fat they've been storing all these years. One

lasting marriage later on in life is infinitely better than one entered into naively early on. Besides, who wants to end up a
starter wife? Just be grateful you're not one of those teenage
brides.

Former PFs

Like John Kerry's career, your past PF is so 2004. And so is his
new fiancée's hairstyle. Take solace, semi-young panicker:
there's no better time to search for an attainable guy than
now. Spotting a former PF in the wedding pages instead of
the crime blotter can be brutal, but it should also spur you to
take action.

Marissa, twenty-eight, doesn't just carry with her the
memory of the moment she found out her ex-PF of two
years got married; she carries around the newspaper clipping
to prove it. It was an aimless Sunday like any other—brunch
with the girls and a debriefing on Saturday night's red-velvet-
roped romp through the city, followed by de rigueur reading
of the Sunday paper. To this day she's still guilt ridden for
releasing those shrieks of horror that rippled throughout
Central Park, scaring helpless children and wildlife, upon discovering Brett's wedding announcement.

Finding out an ex-PF has moved on is a universal experience; we've all been confronted with the reality of a past
PF moving past us. There's nothing worse than the self-
flagellation that occurs, even if you know deep down that he
wasn't the man for you. Why her and not me? What does her
bank account have that mine doesn't? Why does he deserve to
be happy when I'm still out there? But when thrust into this
crushing situation, you have two options: move on yourself, or
be miserable for the rest of your life. I think the choice is clear.

What's particularly salient about this story—besides the
thought of dragging innocent children and wildlife into

Marissa's flirtation with an emotional breakdown—is that it demonstrates how, unless you're willing to spin that negative energy into something actionable, reading the wedding pages can turn you into a marital masochist. And possibly get you booted from Central Park, should policemen arrive on the scene and deem you a security threat. From that moment on, I urged Marissa to take the advice I've offered loved ones for years: you're permitted to read the wedding section on the condition that you transform any jealousy borne out of reading other people's success stories into determination to make a success story of your own.

THE STORY THAT BECOMES A CRUTCH

Even with the emotional trauma that these announcements bring, it's all too easy to hang on to that one story you read about the groom ending the courtship once before three years earlier. He was too emotionally immature at the time, didn't know what he wanted, could never articulate his feelings—and then, after some time, decided to move mountains to be with her, even though by that time she'd already moved on with someone else. But on Valentine's Day when he showed up at her door—after she'd already mourned the passing of Guy #1 and was happily seeing Guy #2—even she couldn't deny the feelings that everyone else was already aware of: she belonged with . . . Guy #1. A story like this can plant a seed of hope in an SPS's psyche that keeps her from moving on. Don't let this happen to you! Nurse these unrealistic expectations only if you want to be miserable—to yourself and those around you—for the rest of your life. Remember, there's a very fine line between being positive and being delusional. Ruth of Charleston, North Carolina, lucked out with this improbably happy ending. You probably will not.

Using Wedding Announcements to Your Advantage

Sabrina, twenty-nine, used her local wedding section as a motivator in her single days. "I didn't find it depressing at all. As a single person, it's encouraging to see all different types of women getting married!" (Right, I'm sure she was this philosophical before she shed her SPS shell.) Instead of fomenting bitterness, Sabrina wisely used these success stories to galvanize her PF search. "Instead of tucking myself away on Sunday mornings in bed reading about other people's happiness, I got out of bed and went to volunteer events, to the gym, and met up with friends so I would feel like I was living my life, not living through other people's lives." And, luckily for Sabrina, it was on one of those Sundays that she decided to check out online dating and met her eventual husband. And wouldn't you know it, she wound up—with excellent placement, no less—on the pages of those same wedding announcements when her own nuptials rolled around.

The Ex Factor: Moving Past Your Old PFs

Yes, everything reminds you of him. The smell in the air, the smell on your pillow, the smell of that old T-shirt of his you've secretly stashed. But clinging to an illusion from the past is not going to help your cause in the present. Reina, thirty, who just got remarried, knows a little something about pressing ahead and burying the past—and that T-shirt—for good. When asked about the difficulty of moving past a painful breakup, she's entirely no-nonsense: "You think you're never going to find that magic again, that you'll never find someone as good—and you know what, you always do."

I've seen too many people—and I add myself to this illustrious list—who voluntarily make themselves prisoners of their own pasts. And without expunging your rewritten memories of him—without wiping off his lingering residue—there's no moving forward. So you must turn the page on past relationships, especially when your past PF is someone else's current husband. Starting now, make it a point to close that formerly pleasant chapter of your life and move on for your own good. Yes, you dated for a year, broke up due to unresolvable issues, but all you can do is cry for a few weeks and move on. End of story.

Yes, we've all suffered those weak moments, wailing about how it would have been our "two-year wedding anniversary had we not broken up three years ago and had he proposed that weekend on Cape Cod and we'd had an abbreviated engagement." Ladies, we all got along great with our former PFs . . . until we broke up. Let's focus on a viable PF in our present!

Have you recently caught yourself saying, "I don't want any hot guys, I want Jon!" when your friends try to convince you what great guys you can catch? Here are the signs you may be hanging on when you should be letting go:

1. "It could have been me! It should have been me!"

Oh, the familiar roars of regret from the SPS who passed up a live one. The day when a PF you passed over gets engaged is a black day indeed. The proclamations of "It should have been me!" have reverberated throughout our inner panic canals for years whenever one of our own has somehow manipulated a man into marrying her. It's painful enough to watch the undeserving ones get engaged in general, but the pain just ricochets that much more when it's to a guy *you* took a pass on! Sure, at the time this guy wasn't worth a second glance, let alone your spit if he were on fire. But now the fact that he proposed to some random girl who inherited him just doesn't sit well at all.

For me, it all started when my friend Jack-Abramoffed me, which is to say he lobbied his ass off for me to go out with a friend of his whose praises he sang in at least six languages. By the time he got to German I was thoroughly turned off and declined his spirited efforts to convince me otherwise. Some months later, the same friend invited me to an engagement party. Naturally I didn't ask who—what's the point? If this guy's off the market, what's a name going to do for me? But guess who was cursing in German when she found out it was *him*? The man I clearly was supposed to have married was now reveling in his new engagement!

Of course I didn't want him then; from everything my friend had described, we were completely incompatible! He was a med student with grueling hours who used his five free hours a week to deplete brain cells with his frat-boy college friends. But now that he's engaged, well, I found myself looking at him with a new set of eyes. He's finished his residency, has bought a new apartment, and apparently has one of those adorable dogs-as-accessories—I felt like I was seeing his whole persona through the prism of an enlightened new reality! If only I could have previewed that ring before, the entire landscape would have changed.

The point is you can no more second-guess your decisions of yesterday than you can go back in time. Berating yourself over a missed opportunity in the past doesn't help your cause—or health—in the present. Besides, our initial instincts are usually right—rest assured there's a good reason you and this guy didn't end up together.

2. "He can register but he can't hide": Tracking Your Newly Engaged Past PF

So it's a sleepy Sunday afternoon, or a desperately lonely Saturday night as it were, and you have the good old Internet as your steadfast companion. You alternate your surfing between CNN and the Wedding Channel Web site. And you almost choke on your economy-sized keg of Cheetos when you stumble across *his* registry. Who has he become and who is this diva with hideous taste in furnishings that he's marrying? A $750 wine rack?! For what? His priceless collection of aged beer bottles? Is JLo getting married again and you don't know about it?! "Ha! No one bought them their last set of flatware! Their wedding's in a week and they have only eleven sets!" you exult.

So if you feel the impulse to check up on him, take a deep breath, step away from the computer, and clear your head. Becoming obsessed by digital sleuthing is not a healthy road to go down. You can reassure yourself that he deserves a woman with no taste in bedding—after all, you could never sleep on (or for that matter, next to) something so unseemly! Thank your lucky stars someone else has the misfortune of marrying a guy who would voluntarily pump more money into the Kate Spade domestics empire and resolve to move on.

3. "I've lost my one true backup!"

The backup: the man you always thought you could fall back on when times got lean and you no longer were. But now your back-burner ex-boyfriend has gotten himself married—that little emotionally stable weasel! You've lost your one true backup, the only last resort you ever thought you could love.

Of course you'd sleep better knowing that you got married before your trusty backup ever could, but you cannot let this news undermine your confidence. Backups can be crutches and inspire laziness—it's easy to get complacent in your search for love if you convince yourself, "It's okay, I can always fall back on Ted; he's not finding anyone either." So instead of wallowing, use this sudden turn of events to spur yourself into action—move forward and get in the game!

Stop the Cycle of Self-Destruction: Learn How to *Finally* Let Go

It all comes back to self-confidence. So your ex-PF's new trophy wife isn't just obnoxiously attractive, but attractively obnoxious (an appeal all its own); it's time to show off *your* new assets: true liberation from a past PF and a healthy sense of all you have to offer. When you have true confidence, people will notice, and reading about those baby brides just won't matter anymore.

Here are some tools to help make moving on a lot smoother:

- If you feel yourself starting to get down, learn how to lean on those who know you better than anyone—your family and friends—and always seem to anesthetize your heartache with a phone call. But avoid those who you know have a propensity for Panic by Proxy!
- Get busy! Sign up for the activities you've always longed to try: becoming a Krav Maga black belt, coaching the Boys Choir of Harlem, or learning Por-

tuguese for the trip to Brazil you've always wanted to take.

- If you're feeling inclined to stalk him via the Internet, get away from the computer for ten minutes— take a walk, take a shower, take that last piece of cake from the fridge if you really need it. Remember to tap the inner strength you possess to move beyond tailing him in his new life.

So, yes, while few can deny that wedding announcements can be a decided mood killer—especially when you read about your ex-PF's wedding—take heart from knowing that the life span of the clipped article is frequently greater than that of the marriages it chronicles. Use it as a catalyst to speed up your dating metabolism—and start digesting the prospect of a new PF. Don't let the ridiculously self-important seriousness of the wedding section weigh down your fighting spirit! Only one more bad date with a self-professed ultimate Frisbee fanatic can do that. And if your backup goes out and gets himself hitched before you do, well, take that as a cue to shift your PF search into high gear.

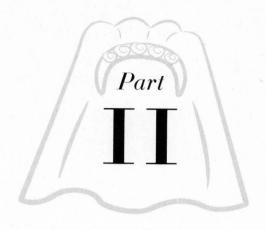

Part

II

You Have Him Right Where

You Want Him:

Stay on Course and You Can

Start Booking Caterers

by the End of the Year

So you've completed Part I, hopefully already feeling ounces lighter from having shed your negative attitude, extricated yourself from negative friends, and dropped some dough on dating sites—all vital steps for a panic-free future! Knowing how to get into the right frame of mind for a PF prowl and how to search judiciously for your ideal PF will be your ticket to entering into an actual relationship with him in Part II. You're already wired with your greatest secret weapons— restored vitality and a new tolerance, not just for PFs who chew their baby corn insufferably slowly, but for those who may not have fit into your old paradigm of perfection. You're on the right path to mental and emotional clarity and nothing—especially not Panic by Proxy or a former PF getting married—is going to interrupt your marriage in the making.

Part II delves deeper into the nuts and bolts of a relationship's inner workings and will help you maintain romantic progress with a well-chosen PF so that you don't, under any circumstances, skid off your marital course. As we established in Part I, a woman's thinly veiled mission to, well, wear a veil is all too easy for a man to detect. The trick is to outsmart the PF and plant the wedding seed in his head as soon as you know you're on fertile ground. If this sounds complicated, think again. After all, how hard is it to outwit and outfox your average man?

This section will be your guide to the next crucial phase of your mission. We'll tackle topics like the first family intermingling (orchestrating every detail, so nothing's left to chance); recommended dating timelines (when to dredge up the painful event from his childhood that forces him to "open up"—happy six-month anniversary); how to ingratiate yourself with his nana without smacking of insincerity; and engagement deal makers and deal breakers (never move for your man!). So as long as you follow along closely, wedding bliss should be a can't-miss. But remember, any minor misstep now can cost you victory in the greater wedding war.

10

Strategy #1: Set—and Stick to—Dating Timelines

As a culture, we are collectively programmed with a results-oriented chip, not a process-oriented one. Though, I should note, I find both expressions equally annoying. The "sport" of any given process is rarely reward enough—and things are no different when it comes to dating. Any sportsman will tell you he's in it to win it, and so are we. As soon as you've fixed your eyes on the PF of your choice, you may metaphorically plant your flag and set about making him yours. In this chapter, we'll learn how the art of setting and sticking to dating time-lines can help you on the road to marriage. We often feel that we are at the mercy of guys, waiting for them to call, waiting for them to ask us to meet their family, and waiting for them to pop the question. But the truth is that *you* can set the tone of the relationship from the beginning. As the architect, you can design your plan and carry it out, according to a well-calculated blueprint.

A Month-to-Month Breakdown
for a Panic-Free Future

No one said your relationship should be laissez-faire. It failed the French and it certainly won't get you married with a lackadaisical PF. You need to campaign for marriage, delicately but decisively! Vive la Panic Revolution!

When the members of my Panic posse ask me the ideal timeline for getting married, I tell them what my therapist told me when my panic kicked into high gear: that there is no "perfect" or "ideal" amount of time. The key is to make sure that the events of your relationship progress in an ideal, or-derly way—a way that brings you closer and leads to mar-riage. Imposing any magic number on the dating timeline puts entirely too much pressure on you and on the relation-ship. You need time to slowly nurture the relationship through all the perils threatening its survival.

It's been indoctrinated into men throughout the ages—scientists believe it's likely through their mothers' breast milk—that they are the prizes, the riches, the spoils, if you will, for which doting SPSs must fight each other. The sooner you ac-cept that—even if you don't want to believe it—the more ef-fectively you can craft your strategy. They wield the power and they know it, even the stupid ones. If he senses any overeagerness, he may start to buckle under the pressure and really become turned off. The last image you want lingering in his mind is the one of you casting a net on your delicate, freewheeling butterfly of a beau.

I've learned the hard way how lightning fast a romance can burn out. For whatever reason, many guys I meet off-handedly confess on our first date that they want to marry me. In fact, I've probably had more first-date proposals than Iran has had human rights violations. But let's be clear, this is the most insidious kind of guy: the one who's so overeager and smitten with you at first that there's nothing left for the romance except an inevitable petering out—and the relation-ship has almost nowhere to go. So ideally, you want to in-trigue him at the outset and then gradually but decidedly grow on him. You want to nurture those early seeds of inter-est carefully and watch something flourish instead of watch-ing already bloomed buds disintegrate with time.

So even though it might seem like you're miles away from the aisle you so badly want to walk down right now, know that the best road to the altar is a slow and steady one. The fol-lowing dating timeline provides tips for each crucial bench-mark of your fledgling relationship and can help you assess where you stand in terms of getting a proposal out of your PF.

Months One and Two:

Ah, the dawn of a new romance—month one and the giddy rush of newness. You're making regular plans, you get a little more physical, and he gets a little more attached. Things are moving smoothly, so it's time to step it up, right? Wrong!

Even if you're dying to break out that salacious French maid's uniform for him, it's all too easy to overdo the domes-tic routine early on. Restrain yourself! Insinuating yourself into his home at this nascent stage—insisting on cooking and hijacking his bathroom counter space with your floral-scented toiletries—reads too easily and will send most guys into their own form of panic. In sprinting that fast coming out of the gate, you reveal your true intentions with exquisite unambiguousness. (The rest of the world knows what your real motives are, but does he have to?)

Yes, you want to do everything you can to make him like you, but earning brownie points is not the same thing as earning respect. Instead, let him earn your kindnesses—this is the stage where he should be solicitous of you! As fun as it is for you to take a completely circuitous route to pick up his dry cleaning while he's playing a round of golf with clients, try to resist the urge. His short-term appreciation will not necessarily translate into long-term reciprocity—at least not yet. In fact, this kind of behavior becomes cloying and more often than not translates into serious bridal backfire.

Although it's often counterintuitive, you want to project reserve in these early stages of the relationship—even if in reality you're feeling just the opposite. You don't want him thinking he already has you in the bag, so keep him on his toes—don't be available *every* single time he asks you out, and above all, keep things light and fun! For God's sake, don't accelerate into the domestic routines of running errands, scrambling eggs, descrambling his illegal cable, or doing laundry together on the weekends—for the first two months you are the kind of girl whose life is way too busy and exciting for such things. At this stage, you should still be dating by candlelight, not by fabric softener.

You're doing great—so keep your cool and just hang in there! You don't advance to months three, six, nine, and the panic-free home stretch without passing months one and two first.

Good signs:

- You've had a great date that does not involve alcohol.
- You speak to him on the phone—not just via text messages—a few times a week.

- You find a bouquet of flowers when you've returned from a weeklong business trip.

Bad signs:

- He gets nervous and agitated if you run into his friends when you're together; once he even introduced you as an out-of-town cousin.
- He still sneaks you in through the service entrance of his building.
- He calls you at random times (in the middle of the workday or late at night) and is evasive about plans.
- He says you should sleep together because he wants to show you an expression of his feelings for you. (If he needs to show you an "expression," let that be a solid commitment—you're obviously not ready for this major step yet.)

Month Three:

At this point, it's likely become increasingly hard to turn the other impossibly high cheekbone on his substandard wardrobe. You have now entered the inevitable gifting-of-the-Banana-Republic-black-silk-blend-sweater-as-wardrobe-staple phase. There's just something about us girls—when we really like someone, we want to shower him with gifts "just because we saw it and we thought of him." As the relationship progresses the urge intensifies, and although it's just as much in your interest as in his that he look presentable, you must resist the urge to give him gifts until he bestows one on you. Your largesse is admirable, but do try to suppress it for the time being. Wait to inaugurate that watershed gift-giving moment until you find yourself saying, "More flowers? I don't have enough vases to keep up with your thoughtfulness" at the very least!

At this point, rather than an all-out gift assault, it's the small gestures that will nudge him to stay the course toward thinking of you as a serious life partner. Is he a sci-fi devotee? If so, suggesting that you hit the *Star Wars* "official" moving exhibit at the convention center will undoubtedly help the force be with you. If you thought listening to the William Shatner CD as background make-out music sufficiently proved your dedication to this relationship, taking the initiative to learn a few words of Klingon so you two can converse more intimately will easily earn you a spot on his nightstand instead of that picture of Princess Leia.

These small gestures will give the relationship the momentum it needs at this crucial do-or-die point. As the first quarter races to a close, recognize that if you are already sputtering along, best to gracefully let it go and try your luck elsewhere. But if all signs point to "Go," feel good about making it to the first big benchmark. Oh, and if you truly think you're up for it, you can now graduate to using "it's me" on his voice mail.

Good signs:

- He introduces you to his friends as his girlfriend.
- You've had sleepovers and you don't feel the need to dive into the bathroom to "freshen up" the moment you wake up. He's seen your morning face and actually thinks it's cute.
- His jewelry gifts say "I love you" even if he can't.

Bad signs:

- His updated Facebook profile says "single and looking."
- You sleep with him even if you're still unsure about your relationship status.
- He still acts cagey on the morning after—and always has an early meeting or breakfast with a client or a date with his personal trainer to rush off to.

Month Six:

"There are two ways to tell how strong a couple is," insists newly married Julie, twenty-eight. "How considerate they are of each other in the morning and how well they get along on vacation." Well, putting on breakfast may not be as easy as putting on your face, but the vacation part can be manipulated easily enough. If you've reached month six and all is well, plan a relaxing four-day getaway (anything longer and he'll breaststroke his way back stateside from Mexico with or without a life vest) for the ideal seed-planting "I want to be with this woman the rest of my life" respite.

If you can manage breakfast, though, great. Now's the time when those little domestic rituals that were so terrifying early on can make him think, "Gee, she's so nice to have around." Take note, however, that this is not about cleaning the toilet or nagging him to help you walk the dog at night. This is about surprising him with a home-cooked meal (even if it's cooked in your favorite restaurant's kitchen), picking up his favorite organic cookies from Whole Foods, or tossing in a few of his shirts when you do laundry.

Good signs:

- He invites you to his work functions.
- You never feel glued to your phone or anxious about him calling.
- You start spending the whole weekend together, just because you both feel like it.

Bad signs:

- You still haven't met his friends—evidence suggesting that you might be merely booty-call material, in which case, it's time you punch out of this relationship for good.

- He seems averse to just "hanging out" and doing everyday things together like running errands, watching TV, etc.

Month Nine:

This is the home stretch; how much do you have left in the tank? You are in! And you'll stay in if you continue to put your best foot forward. This is a very exciting time, since you're "this close" to the one-year mark, making it nearly certain that he's serious about you. The nine-month mark is an important turning point with his friends and family—you're automatically included in most extracurricular activities and you're an overall fixture in his life. You can almost taste success, but be sure not to campaign too hard for a ring right now. In these crucial months, if he sees you're angling too aggressively, it can backfire big-time, so play your hand smartly.

Good signs:

- You attend your first wedding together—and he acts mushy.
- You meet his parents.
- You've uncovered his nerdy secrets that perhaps were best left in the shoebox in his home attic, like his still performing from memory the monologue from *Candide* that he did in acting camp in the fifth grade— and you're still smitten.

Bad signs:

- You're sick and instead of accompanying you to the doctor on a Sunday morning, he sticks cab fare in your pocket and bolts back into bed. This guy's clearly not a supportive partner—and time will not likely make him any more compassionate or attentive.

- He goes stag to his friend's wedding—even though you know the invitation read "and guest."

One Year:

After a year of intense dating, your PF should know you inside and out. But even if you feel like success is close at hand, don't get too complacent. At this seminal point in the relationship, as you get that much more comfortable with him, you'll start to let out your inner bitch occasionally and lapse on good behavior. But meanwhile, he is mentally clocking the countless compromises you'll be making together over a lifetime. If you're too strong-willed/demanding/high-maintenance for your own good, you may earn yourself points in personal pride, but it can likely cost you something bigger: a proposal. A marriage is about compromise—giving in to the little things along the way. And while you don't want to be the only one making sacrifices, doing whatever it takes to make your spouse's life easier will make a fifty-year relationship that much more joyful. So don't be too argumentative and combative when issues arise, as they do in any relationship. Unveiling your well-hidden inner bitch may be a sign you're comfortable with him, but it's a warning sign to him that you could turn at any moment.

Good signs:

- You go on vacation with his family—and it feels really natural.
- You hang out with his friends, even if he's not there.
- He knows your dark sides and is unfazed.

Bad signs:

- He gets weird about giving you a key to his apartment, even though you've made him two copies of

yours. This could hint at possible commitment problems or trust issues.

- After a little tiff about a mixup in your weekend
  plans, he holds a grudge for days.

Two Years:

If you've been dating your boyfriend for more than twenty
months, it's no one's fault but your own. "No emotionally
mature guy will date his girlfriend for more than two years
without proposing," says Felix, twenty-six. "It wouldn't be fair
to drag it out and lead her on. If a guy can't commit by then,
he's wasting her time. You should really know by a year, or else
it's not right." So if you've hit the two-year mark and a proposal still is not materializing, get out sooner rather than later.
Any more time wasted on this guy is robbing you of your real
potential life mate. So don't be afraid to see the situation for
what it is, and move on.

When He Says He's Not the Marrying Kind, Believe Him

If you're like Amber, twenty-nine, who a few years ago
thought her then-boyfriend—who had sworn off the convention of marriage—would have a change of heart, then
you're a fool. "He told me up front that he didn't believe in
marriage . . . They *don't* come around! Trust me," she says.
"You don't want to wait and find that out. Women routinely
put much too much faith in men's ability to change—and
they rarely do." Amber reached her breaking point when her
boyfriend of two years put into writing how thoroughly un-
appealing the prospect of a "formal marriage" was to him.

"He refused to come with me to my best friend's wedding, saying, 'I don't believe in that bullshit,' " she recalls. Eventually he softened, conceding, "I'll get married if it's really that important to you," but that, Amber says, was enough of a clue to escape from the relationship shackles right then and there. She said her gut told her he would never come around. And when she heard he had run back to his ex-girlfriend only to dump her for a second time, she knew her gut was right.

"There's no changing a guy's mind about not wanting to get married in a larger philosophical sense. You can't change people; they can only change themselves," echoes Greg, who's twenty-five and engaged, presumably of his own free will. "Marriage isn't something you can pressure someone into."

Even so, "Most girls I know would not have had the strength to get out of that relationship," Amber contends. Breaking up with someone she loved stung badly, but staying in something that she knew wasn't going anywhere would have been worse.

Michael, thirty-six, actually feels that women's goal of marriage can be an asset when it comes to freeing themselves from dead-end relationships. "Women should be motivated to get out of a stale relationship because of their ticking biological clocks—they don't have time to waste and they know it! If the guy isn't doing what she needs him to do, she should drop him in a second. Men don't have that kind of impetus. I have male friends who've coasted along in casual relationships for years, spending the best years of their lives with women who didn't mean much to them. There's no urgency driving them to make that final break."

Regardless of who leaves the skid marks in the relationship, though, we have only so much time in our lives to waste. To waste it on someone who has no respect for your time or his own is the greatest misjudgment of all.

But You've Put in All This Time—Should You Really Back Out Now?

Sometimes couples are together for so long that any honest evaluation of the relationship gets shelved. At this critical stage, do you really want to start all over again? If you've already run the marathon, wouldn't walking off course in the last fifty feet be considered a grave waste?

Heather, twenty-nine, has stayed with her fiancé for three non-ecstatic years and has recently made the decision to push for a ring because, as she effusively puts it, "it's comfortable with him and I really don't feel like looking for someone else." Her fiancé acquiesced, and now after Heather starts her deep-six-figure job, she will be working enough life-sucking hours at the firm to avoid spending too much time with this man who is passable, but not the love of her life. "I'm going to be working seventy-hour weeks—I'm not going to have time to look for a husband and Jon's already here. Sometimes I feel like I'm settling, asking myself if there's someone better and wondering if he's really 'the one.' But then I figure he could be a lot worse. It's really just a matter of who I found first. What if I don't find someone better? I can't chase an illusion my whole life. I worked three years on this relationship and I'm not going to throw it away," she declared four months before her wedding day.

So shouldn't you see a return on your investment after all this time? Yes, it's true that the longer you date someone, the more intertwined your lives and emotions become. But worse than not being married now is convincing yourself you have to marry this person solely because you put in all this time with him. That's certainly a fate worse than being single. It's even a worse fate than being single with cellulite. So if you reach the two-year mark and you're ready to push, step back and take a hard look at what your real motives are. "I want to marry you for you" can quickly devolve into the less convincing, "I want to marry you because we've already put in two years." And whether it happens consciously or not, you never want to let that factor enter into your equation.

Leslie, now fifty-nine and married for nearly twenty-five years, is a success story along these lines. "I dated someone for three years and not once did it feel right to me," she admits. "Even though I was facing the prospect of becoming an old maid—I was thirty-four at the time, so you can imagine how over-the-hill I felt—I knew I had to break it off. So I did—even though my parents and everyone else thought I was crazy—and then I met my husband, who I dated for twenty-five days before we got engaged. I knew he was the one from the beginning. I'm so glad I didn't stick it out with my other boyfriend just because I invested all that time, like I know a lot of women would have."

Ultimatums: The Panicker's Last Bargaining Chip

If you give him an ultimatum, I swear I will stop writing this book righ—See? I caved. You knew it and I knew it. I have no willpower to carry out my own bluff—and neither do you. Issuing an ultimatum can be tricky and often backfires, drives away your PF, scrambles your cable connection, makes you gain fifteen pounds in your ankles, and is simply not good form. When you back someone against a wall, you may not like the result. If you choose to strong-arm your PF, don't be surprised when he doesn't automatically crumble like a house of cards. If you're going to make wild threats, you better be prepared to back them up; and rare is the woman who has the strength of will to follow through on her own ultimatum.

Jessica, twenty-eight, is no stranger to ultimatums. In fact, it's an ultimatum that she cites as the saving grace from what could have been an imperiled life as a permanent girlfriend. Sam, twenty-nine, her now-fiancé, was an indefatigable dater and loved every noncommittal minute of it. So how did this SPS climbing up a down escalator not only survive, but succeed? After two years of dating and one year of cohabitating, she issued an ultimatum that Sam ultimately succumbed to. "You've got to throw your chips on the table; if you don't set a deadline, then it's giving them all this time for free," Jessica opines. "If I didn't lay down the law when I did and give him a firm deadline at the end of one full year of living together, I'd still be dating him—probably until I was 35!"

Sam, on the other hand, admits some misgivings. "I resent her for pressuring me to propose; what's a confession under duress really worth?" he asked. "She took the fun out of it for me." Yet Sam caved in to the prevailing pressure, despite his emotional misgivings, because, as he remembers it, "I wasn't quite ready to marry her, but I didn't want to lose her, either." And so with the proverbial knife to his throat, Sam proposed just before the deadline expired. While Jessica knows that Sam resents the fact that she pressured him, she still maintains that she did what was in her—and their relationship's—best interest. "He hemmed and hawed for so long that he needed a huge push or else he never would have done it on his own." While happily married *now*, Sam confided that he is nervously awaiting the next ultimatum—when to have kids, when to move to the suburbs—because, as he sees it, "why would the ultimatums ever stop?"

Clearly, there are instances in which ultimatums work— PFs do cave under the pressure, just as detainees mercifully buckle at Guantánamo Bay—but it's up to you to decide if that's how you want your proposal to come about. If you feel he needs that extra nudge—that he otherwise wouldn't budge even though he is deeply committed to you and your future together—then extorting the proposal through an ultimatum may be the right course of action for you. Just make sure that at the end of the day you're really getting everything you want. A proposal without the certainty and emotion behind it may not be enough.

Ultimatums: The Final Analysis

Ultimately, I don't believe in epic romances. At least not in ones without some level of commitment beyond "Come on, babe, you know how much I love you—how else can I prove it to you?" Well, my answer to that almost rhetorical question is simple: put your matrimony where your mouth is!

It's the common sense test: if you feel it's taking too long or he's too unsure, listen to your inner voice. However, the simplest and often truest test of all is if you really love someone, you'll want to be with that person for the rest of your life. If he really loves you, how much more time does he really need? Another three years to see how much *more* he can love you? "I love you, but I want to make sure I *really* love you"?! If he loves you, he loves you and he'll want to get married.

I've met girls who have conditioned themselves into blindly believing their lollygagging PFs, who assure them that it's going to "work out," to "just give it some time," that it will happen "sooner rather than later." But one feels compelled to ask just what "some more time" really means. Why shouldn't his words run his actions? This resonant and relevant quote says a mouthful: "Men in relationships should be treated like silent movies. Pay attention to what they do, not what they say"—meaning talk is very cheap.

Jessica, our friend who doles out ultimatums, naturally

has her own opinions. She estimates that the "shopportunity" cost—the reduced chance to meet other guys—for the average woman is staggering, claiming that women typically miss out on meeting one hundred men a year while toiling with a guy with dwindling dedication. Now that's a sobering thought. "You have to look out for yourself," she says. "No one else is looking out for your best interests. So if you're sticking to one man, something has to come out of that sacrifice of being with him."

Perhaps if you're using phrases like "sacrifice of being with him," then you're already taking a heavy chance spending time with him in the first place. But remember, while time frames present a general outline for a courtship leading up to marriage, you are going to have to trust your intuition about whether or not your PF is the right one—and very likely, the "right one" is one for whom the concept of marriage isn't such a hard sell.

Following the timelines outlined in this chapter will help you lay the groundwork for a proposal—one that's of his own accord. Only you can determine for yourself if and when there's a right time to walk away, but sticking to the game plan should bring about a proposal naturally—if he is the man you're meant to marry.

11

Strategy #2: Be "Supportive" of His Relationship with His Mom

Early on in your relationship, the most important relationship of his to zero in on—and one that's ultimately way more telling than the maternal way he cradles his newborn baby BlackBerry weighing in at a shockingly low 4.5 ounces—is the one he has with his mother. Observe every phone call: is he an I-love-you-Mommy kind of guy, practically curling up in a fetal position during every conversation? Does he still drop his laundry off at home on the weekends and get a particular kick out of mommy using fabric softener on his Underoos? If so, you'll want to capitalize on the situation and start setting boundaries now. You've got to carve out a leading role for yourself in this special mother–son oedipal freak show before it's too late.

This chapter explores the ugly side (as if there's any other kind) of dating a micromanaged mama's boy: what are the warning signs? How will it inevitably bleed into your relationship with him? And what does it all mean for your matrimonial future? You'll acquire tools from former SPSs to help you stay strong when pitted against his even stronger-willed Mother Smotherer, make—or at least fake—peace with her, and secure a smooth first family intermingling. If there's one thing that can impede the advancement of your relationship or a proposal, it's his mom—so here's how to make sure you're never competing for first place in your PF's world.

Too Close for Comfort

He twirls the ringlets of her hair with more sexual excitement than when twirling you on top of him. His kisses her on the lips and you're wondering why it seems to convey more passion than the two of you have generated lately. So what's the story here—is he dating you or his mother?!

One of my past PFs seemed to have it all. He was charming, disarming, and very successful—but had all the classic symptoms of the micromanaged mama's boy. It took a while for me to sort through the situation—was it really as bad as I feared?

Being second to his mom in the kitchen was one insult I could swallow with grace. But getting one-upped in the bedroom is something nary a couple's counselor or exorcism could smooth over! When trying to coax my PF out of bed one morning, I figured I'd be met with the usual early-morning protests. Instead, I opened a profoundly disturbing Pandora's box. Hoping he'd respond to more aggressive measures, I started gingerly stroking him in some of his favorite places. He liked it and I was feeling pleased with myself until he mumbled, "Mom, just another minute, okay?" Horrified, I shook him awake. "Oh, Doree . . ." Turns out, I didn't need to make him any eggs for breakfast; he could just eat the ones on his face. But the situation really raised the question, Where did I fit into this family of his? As a glass-half-fuller, I rationalized it, convinced myself it was still better than him screaming out an ex-girlfriend's name at an inopportune time. But the grim reality was impossible for me to ignore: my perennial competition would always be the same one person—his mother.

When I broached the lifetime role of baby babushka that he plays like a pro, he went into defensive mode. "I'm her baby boy, what do you expect?" he sheepishly offered.

"Her baby boy is twenty-seven!" I snapped.

What was I thinking? Of course a twenty-seven-year-old, 170-pound banker is still his mother's baby boy. Until three years ago, she still considered him in utero. Thank goodness she gave him the okay to cross the street alone without a helmet two years earlier—or the entire landscape of our relationship would have changed!

So take heed: your PF's relationship with his mother may not be his best selling point. Here are some of the warning signs that indicate you might be dealing with a baby boy yourself:

Warning Sign #1: You're a Permanent Second-Place Finish

It doesn't get much freakier than when your PF reverentially sings the praises of his mom's sumptuous silhouette. "My dad really lucked out with my mom!" my past PF loved to gush.

"She was four foot eleven, a double D, and ninety-eight pounds when they got married." And then there was the woman's penchant for Soviet bloc cooking? No top-rated restaurant this side of Siberia could match her culinary chops, according to my PF. So was I intimidated? Maybe a little, the way a paddleball player might be intimidated playing against Andre Agassi. After all, what Long Island–bred panicker has the wherewithal to make blini from scratch?

But I had to remember: the secret lies not in trying to one-up your PF's mom—no one can ever replace or match his wretched old (milk) maid—but instead in trying to create your own specialties, edible and otherwise, that he'll come to crave as much as that blini special.

Warning Sign #2: You're Not the First Person He Turns To

Flagging down a cab with one hand and dialing the doctor's office with the other, I was awfully close to getting my PF the medical attention he needed when he was writhing in pain from an acute ear infection. Until he called his mother.

"No, no, no, you pour some hydrogen peroxide in your ear!" I heard her bark at him through the phone. "That's how you clear this up! You don't need the doctor."

"Um, if you want to disinfect your ear hair, perhaps," I countered, sensing an imminent power struggle. "I think you really need to see a doctor now." But my PF, being a man, and thus incapable of making a decision for himself, was collapsing under the weight of indecision, conflicted over whether to trust the woman whose bosom he'd suckled from birth to age two or the woman whose bosom he'd been suckling for the past six months. And sure enough, ten minutes later we darted into CVS and emerged with the trusted brown bottle of hydrogen peroxide. Ida, one, Doree, nyet.

Part of cultivating a lasting relationship is caring for and relying on each other in times of need. If his mom is presenting a major roadblock every time you have an opportunity to showcase that rare nurturing side, it's going to be a problem—because he'll sure have a hard time committing unless he truly believes he *needs* you at his side. Confronting your PF about his overdependence on his mom for every minute decision—and getting him to acknowledge the problem—is crucial; slowly but surely, he'll start to turn to you first in his times of need—as he should.

Warning Sign #3: She Interrupts Your Dates

You're on a first date with a guy when his pants start lighting up and vibrating—normally a sign the date's going well. But not this time: "Hi, Mom!" he cackles excitedly into the cell phone, without much reserve. You butter your bread while she's clearly buttering his, and all you hear is:

"Yeah, I'm with her now."

"Appetizers."

"Maybe in two hours or so."

"Okay, I'll call you then. Love you!"

And just like that, the *Modern Bride* magazine in your head slams shut. Any so-called man who feels compelled to debrief his mom on the date he's going on—while he's on it!—should rightfully tip you off to his questionable stability. Even though it might seem too early in the relationship to be drawing conclusions, don't forget that his relationship with her will affect you in every way: arriving late for dates because he's been lingering at her house, or trying to muzzle you during family visits because he fears your steadfast lefty leanings will clash with her own political views can grate on the SPS with even the most saintly patience. If he can't get through a date without calling her, singing her praises, or picking up when she calls, it's probably a good idea to take your exit and leave him with the woman he clearly loves the most.

Warning Sign #4: She Thinks He's God

Megalomaniac sons and the doting mothers who smother them—it's tough to know what to do when you're trapped in the middle of an oedipal lovefest. I've met mothers of every stripe in my day, and whatever corner of the world she hails from, your PF's mother will always gush with unabashed glee over her pride and joy of a child—your PF. It's always the same maternal party line: "My son, the doctor." "My son, the lawyer." "My son, the acclaimed subway performance artist!" There's no one better than him. And no one good enough. Not even you. (Especially not you.)

However, the underlying danger here is that her overzealous and unconditional approval may have actually convinced him that he is in fact God's gift to the world—and this can spell doom for your relationship. Good luck trying to have an equal, loving partnership with someone who's never wrong. It's unfortunate, but this mother–son relationship is so firmly established, there's no way even your determined force can penetrate these walls. The son of a Mother Smotherer is unlikely to cede to your needs or compromise—and is this really the kind of future you envision? You don't want to spend years of your life trying to legislate power over your own relationship. Remember: without his mother and her bullhorn, a megalomaniac is just a bullshitter without the goods. Ultimately, you must forsake this false messiah to let him be with his most steadfast worshipper.

MOTHER SMOTHERERS: THE CLASSIC PARADOX

As desperately as many of them want their baby boys to find a worthy wife, a mother often turns on a dime once she detects even the faintest whiff of a girl spiriting away her precious progeny. This paradox is embodied in widescreen format in my Aunt Sunny. Sunny would reveal her natural hair color if it meant getting my cousin Jeff married; and while she ardently proclaims that "no one is good enough for her Jeffrey," in one breath, in the next she'll declare that "Jeffrey needs to find a nice girl and get married." As in:

12:53 p.m.: "Why can't my Jeffrey find a nice girl to give me some grandchildren?"

12:54 p.m.: "They're all loose gold diggers! My Jeffrey isn't going to marry any slut!"

12:55 p.m.: "Barbara, you don't know any thin girls from the temple?"

"She needs final approval because she feels she's being replaced," Jeff helplessly notes. In a lose–lose situation like this one, it can take an especially hard toll on the guy. Poor Jeff's practically given up on dating—it's just easier that way.

Meeting His Mom for the First Time

Some PFs' spines simply have the strength of a pipe cleaner, and they feel the need to bring you home to solicit their mother's opinion before they set their own clay of opinion to dry in the kiln. This is the PF who also has a front-row pew at the Church of Motherly Chokehold and won't date anyone his mom doesn't want praying there. So when gearing up for your visit, be prepared to be both pleasant and confident, and ready to stand your ground. Just know that anyone can hold court with the queen mother—you just have to make it absolutely clear that you recognize the real jewel in her crown: her (semiprecious) son.

During the inaugural visit:

- Assert yourself, but not in an abrasive manner. Let it be known you're a strong-willed woman, but not one who's too strident to stomach an afternoon of coffee, or the nauseatingly cute stories about your PF when he was the world's most perfect baby boy.
- While she might act like a dictator, now's the time to show her you're not a doormat. If she's ordering you around the house like hired help: "Chloe, would you mind taking a look at the air conditioner—it's on the fritz today," calmly tell her you left your tool belt at home and maybe she should call a professional.
- Compliment her, the house, and anything that is or isn't nailed down (especially the sizable collection of Hummel figurines in the living room) to put her at ease and appeal to her aesthetic sensibilities.
- If you anticipate a potential battle brewing, skillfully shift the topic to something more neutral.

Starting off on a good note with his mom is vital to your relationship's future. He's praying that the two of you will get along and that no altercations brew, so if you do feel the need to rifle through her medicine cabinet, at least hold off on

switching labels on the bottles. The first impression is an in-
delible one for most people, so adopting a positive attitude is
crucial to your first interaction. This can most definitely work
to your advantage: when your PF sees the effort you're making with his mom, he'll know that you are someone he can
have around his family—for the long haul.

Carving Out a Peace Accord

Learning how to walk that delicate tightrope—mastering that
perennial dance between the two of you and his mother—
may be one of the greatest trials of your relationship. And
while you want to set strict boundaries with your PF and ensure that he's always in your court, certain small political gestures can help smooth over a delicate situation. His mother
certainly isn't rushing to abdicate power to you, but if you let
her *think* that she has somewhat of a role, it can make everyone's life infinitely easier.

Soliciting her advice on the benign things—asking what
gift to get your PF for his birthday or getting the recipe for
her famous guacamole—is a great way to start cultivating an
amicable relationship. Your guy can also be instrumental in
this department by conveying how much you respect her:
"Mom, Rena's trying to polish her résumé and wants to know
if you wouldn't mind taking a look at it," he could say to make
the retired English teacher feel useful and appreciated.

The least you can do is try to fashion a resolution—for his
sake and your sanity! No one loathes moral lessons more than
I do (watching *7th Heaven* was a form of torture for me), but
making compromises and adjustments is one of the realities of
a relationship and of preparing yourself for the daily give-and-
take of marriage. Expending precious mental energy on her

and draining even more of it neutralizing her relationship poison is probably even less fun than it sounds like, but you and your PF can always turn the tide of her fierce currents.

By all means, unleash your pent-up frustration—just not to her face. After all, there's no shortage of people in your life who will gladly listen to your venting sessions—your own family, friends, and neighbors in her community who I'm sure have a voracious appetite for this kind of trash-talking junk food fodder. And try to keep it in check with your PF— don't be a pushover, but do choose your battles carefully when it comes to her. She is still his mom, after all.

If the Pot Boils Over

Rebounding from any contretemps with his mom requires delicate grace—you never want to admit defeat, but you'll be damned if she squeezes a postmatch handshake out of you. But whoever gets bragging rights to the match, remember that you still need to maintain some semblance of a warm relationship with her; if things are frosty, everyone around you feels uncomfortable and won't necessarily prompt your PF to invite you to important functions, like anniversary parties or grandparents' milestone birthdays.

But it's completely understandable that the ferocious barking of a pit bull can take its toll, even for the most steeled woman. For example, his mom slyly asks about your middling acting career. "So, what's your Plan B if this acting thing falls through?" she scoffs. You try to exercise restraint, but end up snapping back: "I'm surprised you care so much about my career—weren't you a stay-at-home mom your whole life?"

Awkward.

Now you're the Monday-morning quarterback and you must figure out how to recover from this showdown. Avoidance is fun for only so long. You need to address the issues before they really fester. You don't want to deepen any dissent between you and your guy by arguing with her, but you shouldn't have to take her pointed potshots either. In order to resolve this nasty flare-up—and avoid risking a permanent grudge—you must try to stop the heavy bleeding as soon as possible.

Even if you have every reason to arch your back, holding on to hostility will only alienate you from the rest of his family, and especially from your PF. The only viable option is to confront your guy—explain how frustrated you feel by his mother constantly undermining you, but assure him that you want to mend things—and hope that he has enough respect for you and your relationship to try to help smooth things over. He will need to work on his mom before she sharpens any more of her knives; laying down the law with her, he should tell her how much pride you take in your career and that she needs to taper her negativity and disapproval of your career choice. At the same time, he has to serve as your support system when you feel like you're about to blow. His role should be that of the go-between, so that as you and his mom get more comfortable with each other being in the picture, future exchanges will be much more pleasant and stress-reliever balls will be optional.

Drawing the Line

Sometimes, the son also rises. So if you really feel that this PF and your relationship are worth fighting for, and his mom shows no signs of slowing down, you may need to summon your courage and draw the line—even if it means risking your relationship.

Lindsey and Paul are happily engaged, save for the one Achilles' heel of their otherwise idyllic relationship: Paul's mother, Arlene, whom Lindsey considers to have all the warmth of shoe polish, and who makes Lindsey feel like an easy target. Whereas Paul can do no wrong in Arlene's eyes, Lindsey can do no right. Rising interest rates? It's that menacing little Lindsey! Twenty-minute previews at the movies? Lindsey's prints are all over it! "I've changed her name in my mind," says Lindsey with that naughty look that a child gets when he's just copped some cookies when no one was looking. "She's now known as PIA—Pain in the Ass—to me and Paul. I think it suits her."

In fact, last Christmas, Lindsey recalls getting a holiday card in the mail from Arlene with a picture of the whole family, including Paul's brother and his own family. "It took me a few seconds, but I realized that she'd cut out her other son's wife—she's a maniac!" she recalls. "She's horrible to no one else but me and her daughter-in-law; she's more in love with her sons than her husband—she's obsessed with them!" says Lindsey. "This was honestly my biggest worry about marrying him," she confesses. "Paul has always insisted that if I have an issue with her, all I have to do is tell him and he'll take care of it, but this was still a big problem hanging over our heads." PIA unleashed her uncommon wrath toward Lindsey without ever coming up for air, and finally Lindsey reached her breaking point.

She wasn't about to buckle to the ill-intentioned bitch, so she finally took the most direct approach to this mighty test and laid it on the line for Paul: it was either his mother or

her—he would have to choose his allegiance. Faced with losing the woman he loved, Paul was left no choice but to cut off
the toxicity at the source. He gave Arlene two options: either
accept Lindsey or be sliced from his life if she didn't. Lindsey,
of course, was secretly hoping for the latter so that she'd be
free of PIA permanently, but in true PIA form, Arlene acquiesced at the eleventh hour.

In the end, Paul demonstrated exactly where his loyalty
lay: he firmly told Arlene that if she continued to try to inter-
vene in any of their closed-door decision making or upset
Lindsey with petty, undercutting comments, she would alienate herself from her favorite son too. Lindsey stood her
ground and it paid off because Paul proved himself worthy of
a lifetime commitment. Ultimately, what had been two minutes away from permanently torpedoing their relationship
wound up fusing them even closer together. "When Paul
stood up for me, it made all the difference," Lindsey said. "I
knew that I had been right to stick with him. But I was also
right to stick up for myself."

Clarissa, twenty-nine, was already engaged when she
found herself in a similar situation. Trying painstakingly not to
step on her future mother-in-law's toes—let alone kick her in
her paunchy stomach—Clarissa steadied herself every time
the woman opined on areas over which she has no jurisdic-
tion, like, for instance, which method of birth control Clarissa
was using. "I'm really trying my hardest not to tangle with her
before the wedding," Clarissa told me at the time. "But she
has not made it easy."

Her fiancé, Jason, was so terrified of his mother that during the dreaded Thanksgiving holiday, he took the cake for
exacerbated White Man's Guilt. He felt it necessary to lie to
his mother, claiming he was on call in the hospital, instead of

standing up to her and admitting that he was spending Thanksgiving with Clarissa's family this year. Understandably annoyed, Clarissa wondered what this hinted for their future together if he couldn't assert himself over an issue so minor? Jason didn't need to simply stand up to his mom—he was in desperate need of a spine transplant!

That Jason made it to her family's for Thanksgiving unscathed was beside the point. Clarissa finally concluded that she wanted a forthright husband, not a milquetoast happy to circumvent an issue that would only creep up again and again rather than addressing it head-on. She confronted him and let him know that if he wanted their wedding to move forward, changes had to be made. They ultimately agreed that no matter what they decided about holidays or any other events in the future, he would tell—not ask—his mom, whether she liked it or not.

As Lindsey and Clarissa well know, if you weaken your position of power now, you're giving her free rein to forever sidestep you. Even if a volcanic fight erupts—lava shooting everywhere—pitting you against the Beast, remember that *you* are the plucky bride-to-be and that if you are going to marry this PF and, by extension, this family, then you have to set parameters—and fast. When you talk to your PF, convey to him the importance of taking a stand against his mother and supporting his future wife, with whom his loyalty should ultimately lie. And as her son, he needs to be the one to step up and defend you and draw the line—not you.

Solid relationships and mutual respect are born from setting boundaries and asserting yourself when needed, so don't be afraid to take issue with your PF and attack this third rail of your relationship head on.

When Both Sides Collide: What to Do the First Time Your Families Intermingle

Now that your own relationship with his mother is as contained as North Korea's nuclear weapons, it's time to determine the course of action for the inevitable family intermingling. Just because you're dreading a clash of fighting factions, don't call off the all-important family introductions and the subsequent trip to New England! This is a crucial step on the path to marriage and besides, if you call it off, how else will you get to see what real life Connecticut WASPs look like up close?

Instead, plan for a no-fail afternoon; orchestrate every detail, leaving no room for matrimonial derailment. You want to muzzle grandpa, replace mom's cooking with catering, comb through the prefab topics, and pray for a divine miracle to take care of the rest.

Gena, thirty, looked forward to conjoining both sets of families about as much as a discourse on prescription meds from Tom Cruise. "Both our dads are doctors and our moms are interior decorators, so I think they'll have enough to talk about initially, but once things digress from work, all hell might break loose," she fretted.

When his mother, the Ogre, as Gena lovingly refers to her, and her own mom finally sat down together, the clans clashed almost immediately. The Ogre fired off, "When am I going to get a grandchild already?" to which Gena's mom tried to suppress the urge to say, "When your lazy son gets his act together and proposes while her eggs are still good!" Things really turned ugly when the Ogre commented on what a lovely home Gena's mom had "for someone of obviously modest means." But because Gena and her guy discussed in advance how to diffuse any potential bomb during the visit, she artfully managed to steer the conversation toward the safe subjects she knew both sets of parents would be comfortable with (for example, both grew up in Brooklyn and still have a strong attachment to it)—and the rest of the day went off without a hitch (except for a playful rumble over New York's best baseball team).

How to Ensure a Rumble-Free Family Gathering

The undercutting barbs don't have to fly between your families if you take measures to set the right tone for the day.

- Prep your parents on his set's likes and dislikes: if you know she's a gay marriage activist, a nice gesture would be to subtly garnish your meal with oranges—the citrus fruit long associated with gay rights (and certainly a refreshing snack on a summer day!).
- Suggest a neutral spot—not someone's home—such as a cute, midpriced restaurant to take the pressure off. (Added bonus: in public, there are too many witnesses to create any police-worthy commotion.)
- To ensure everyone's nice and relaxed, a bottle of wine—not an open bar—can do just the trick.
- You know his father is traveling to Brazil next month? How about suggesting your parents bring a few of their pics from their own trip to the rainforests?
- Just remember how far a little thoughtfulness and restraint go in situations like these.

"How a man treats his mother is usually a good indication of how he'll treat you." Keep thinking this will happen and I'll see you at the altar when O.J. finds the real killer. Sure, we all melt when we see how attentive he is to his sweet ole mom—calling every day, visiting on the weekends, and helping her with the shopping. But what seems so cute at first wears off pretty fast—especially when you take a backseat to *her* needs. That attentiveness doesn't necessarily shift from her to you just because you're dating. She's not going anywhere—unless you have a New Jersey uncle in "waste management" who can help you out.

Know this: if you and your PF have a truly rosy future together, at some point *your* needs should start coming first. So if the strategies outlined in this chapter don't work, you should relegate this PF to NBNMM (nice, but not marriage material) and move on to one who's less micromanaged for your own sanity, as devotion like that rarely dissipates!

12

Strategy #3: Never Move in Together Before You Get the Ring

Most relationships will reach that unavoidable point during which the dreaded topic of bridging homes comes up. But heed this advice: don't move anywhere for your man unless your ring finger is getting a sizable workout from Tiff's. There can be no negotiation on this point. The worst mistake a rookie panicker in love can make is to follow her PF to his new home, whether it's across the street or across the Pond. No matter how "exotic" the idea of following him to a locale where trans fat is considered a luxury item, it's not the bridge that leads to marriage on the other side. Moving for him before matrimony only spells out your relationship's impermanence and puts undue stress on a romance that under other circumstances might continue to flourish. There's no faster way to sabotage your potential engagement than moving for

your guy—except, of course, letting him glimpse you in natural daylight after your waxer's been out of the country for
two months. Damn Helga and her ill Czech aunt!

In this chapter, we will take a closer look at why moving
for him or moving in with him doesn't translate into marrying him; the smoke screen that is cohabitation; and the tools
you can use to take a stand against his intransigence.

California Dreaming . . . Turned Nightmare

Cassie, twenty-six, now relocated to L.A., found herself up-
rooted to the land of organic dog food and dry cleaners during her own pursuit of marriage. An SPS can mask her veiled
intentions all she wants, but it's clear as day that when an SPS
moves for her man, it's not "to try a new adventure and step
out of my comfort zone"—a flimsy excuse that even a novice
panicker wouldn't buy. Deluded SPSs can convince themselves of anything and Cassie's boyfriend at the time cajoled
her to uproot her well-established and mostly fulfilling life on
the East Coast for the smoggier skies of L.A., a leap of faith
she's deeply ruing right now.

Expecting an imminent engagement once she'd settled
in—they all do—Cassie instead found herself completely
blindsided. Three months after she'd arrived, she unexpectedly
awakened with a shudder in the middle of the night, not to a
drugged-up, gun-wielding burglar (which she might have pre-
ferred), but to skid marks left by the live-in boyfriend, who was
fleeing in the dark. He couldn't summon the spine to admit his
misgivings when she arrived, and there was no good-bye, no
breakup talk, not even the courtesy to leave any organic dog
food for Cody, who, incidentally, he took with him.

So instead of the man she thought she would marry, the life she thought she'd be able to carve out for herself in an especially plasticky section of plastic West Hollywood, Cassie was left alone with heightened Panic and without any miniature dog-cum-accessory like all those other women carry to keep them company.

Why Is Moving for Your Man the Marital Kiss of Death?

If your motive is marriage, never, under any circumstances, move for him unless you know the ring is cooling its heels in some sock drawer, waiting for the right moment to reveal itself. Uprooting your life for someone who has clearly decided to put his needs above yours by moving away from you in the first place is setting yourself up for spectacular disappointment.

You should never live under the same roof with your guy before getting hitched in any case (more on that below), but moving cities or even states to do so can get you into real trouble. You can easily wind up entangled in a situation where you are dependent on your PF financially and for shelter—something that does not scream autonomy. And nothing puts greater stress on a relationship than when one person has to assume responsibility for the other. You should value maintaining your independence at all times, no matter what your relationship stage or age. You are nothing if not self-reliant.

Isabelle, twenty-six, learned that the hard way when she moved from Boston to Portland to join her PF. They had met during graduate school while spending a semester in Latin America—and Isabelle was certain he was the one. "When I finished my program, I moved out to join him since he still had another year of school. We moved in together and I thought it was going to be so great. We never actually talked about marriage, but I assumed it was in the cards because we talked about all sorts of other plans—going back to Panama to work, and then maybe a year in Providence, where my family's from."

But Portland was not the dream destination Isabelle had hoped for. Having left all her friends and family on the East Coast, she arrived to find her PF ensconced in his schoolwork with very little time or inclination to help her make friends or settle in. "He sort of left me to fend for myself while he went on about the life he'd been living for years. I was jobless, with no support system, and it put an enormous strain on our relationship. Here I'd envisioned us happily setting up house and picking out dishware at Crate and Barrel—but now it was clear he'd wanted me to move to make things convenient for him, not because he was really interested in building a life together."

Another pitfall of the disastrous early move is that you will also feel shamed and disgraced when you return home to live in your parents' musty basement—or charming alcove studio for one, as you desperately try to spin it—empty-handed and heartbroken after the relationship's eventual failure. "Nothing was harder than admitting it hadn't worked and moving back home," Isabelle recalls. "I even stuck it out in Portland for another year after we broke up, just because I was so ashamed. I told everyone I really liked it there, but I was miserable and in reality, I just couldn't face telling all the friends I'd crowed to about this fabulous guy that I'd made a mistake."

WHY LONG-DISTANCE RELATIONSHIPS
ARE A LITERAL LONG SHOT

If you rightly decide to hold your ground, be wary of the next option he might impose on you: the long-distance relationship. When dating long distance, it's often more than mere physical distance that separates you: it's mental, psychological, and emotional distance too. Distance in every sense of the word. This makes it almost impossible for any relationship to evolve, and you will inevitably find yourself alone admiring the Space Needle on Saturday nights, wondering why, if you have a boyfriend, he's not there with you. These cross-country booty calls might be fun for a while, but how can the relationship withstand so many obstacles, especially after so many rounds of bad "plane hair"?

If one of you is compelled to move away for any reason, it's essential to talk about the fate of your relationship now rather than later. With your marriage clock ticking, you don't want to waste time with a PF who isn't actually present. Furthermore, it's just the law of human nature that guys seem to have a much easier time finding other female forms of distraction if their number one woman isn't right in front of their face. If you're long distance, the inevitability of breaking up is always looming large.

Romantic Roommates Without
the Responsibility

If a relationship's mettle really needs to be tested in a cohabitation situation, it boils down to a stunning lack of trust on one or both of your parts. You don't feel fully secure and con-

fident in the relationship and are seeking some sort of confirmation that you think will come from living together before
marriage. If you think cohabitation will bring you closer to
your desired destination—the altar—you are deluding yourself. Here's why.

   When problems arise—substantive ones, like debates over
the proper way to load towels in a washing machine—the
couple that is test-driving marriage through this video game
simulator is more likely to chalk it up to incompatibility than
to what it really is: one of those meaningless dustups that are
part of daily life and occur between even the happiest of
married couples. When you're married, you are that much
more committed—to the institution of marriage and to each
other—and you're not going to throw in the towel (white
ones go in a separate load, for the record) as readily as you
would if you were living together without a ring. The situation is recognized for what it is—a silly tiff about towels. But
if you haven't already taken the steps to commit, these instances can take on a disproportionate significance as he finds
himself thinking, "Can I really handle being with someone
who turns into a fascist when I'm doing laundry?"

   A friend recently told me that he moved in with his girlfriend and was going to give it what he estimated to be a six-
month test period, after which he would evaluate how "easy"
it was to live together in order to finalize his decision to propose. He thought he had it all figured out, but his language only
underscores just how clueless he is about relationships and the
essence of marriage. That he even injected the word *easy*
alerted me to the fact that he doesn't have the first clue about
the stuff of which a good marriage is made. No matter how
seemingly "easy" something may be, that certainly isn't the
barometer for a healthy relationship—it's simply the barometer for his low standards of success.

Mina, twenty-nine, cohabitating with her PF pre-engage-
ment, shares her wealth of experience with her spinsterly sisters. Admittedly nervous about living together before she got
the ring, Mina feared what most girls do—that he might get
too comfortable and languish indefinitely in that comfort
zone. "Dave had a talk with my mom and promised her . . ."
Well, if he promised the mother, then by all means! "Now
we're online picking out wedding invitations with one minor
detail missing; well, not that minor. Just the engagement part,"
Mina says sheepishly.

"I never wanted to become one of those girls who was
pushing for the ring," she continues, "but there are genuine
logistical factors here. My grandparents are old and I really
wanted them at our wedding." But Dave had a piercing coun-
terargument (they all do): "This isn't about logistics. Getting
married is about us, babe," he'd "reassure" her.

Women need to be aware that almost all commitment-
phobic men in this situation can easily manipulate the conversation so they end up looking like the good guy. They
won't reflexively bristle at your concerns and will appear
reasonable, even sensitive. This is especially tricky because
moving in together *does* seem like a step forward. But it all de-
pends on his intentions.

When Dave finally proposed after three months of living
together, it was not a moment too soon for Mina. "Looking
back on it, I didn't love having that antsy feeling all the time,"
Mina says, recalling the waves of anxiety that crashed over her
even before the boxes were unpacked. "From the first day I
moved in, I felt impatient and agitated. I spent a lot of time
worrying during those initial months about whether I was
doing something that would make him change his mind. I
believed he was sincere in his intentions for our relationship,

but I have plenty of friends for whom the situation has gone the other way."

So what exactly was Dave looking for in living with Mina? What tangible sign or confirmation was he expecting to see? "I don't know if he even knew what his expectations were in living together. I think he was looking for more of an overall feeling, instead of looking for any specific thing," she concludes. I think we have a new winner for the embodiment of hazy postmodern bullshit reasoning about relationships.

Just remember—living together before marriage is always a test-drive, which on some level means he's not sure. And if he's not sure, you don't have the time or energy for that.

Why Living Together Can Spell Out Your Domestic Doom

The idea that living with your PF will "bring you closer to your partner" or that it surely bespeaks marriage is faulty logic, mostly trumpeted by the younger generation of early-twenty-something girls. Chalk it up to a kind of naive idealism about relationships, but they perpetuate and reinforce it among themselves to such a degree that almost all young women today will fall into that trap at least once and cave in under the avalanche of their own self-delusion. I tell them that if they actually want their long-term plans with their PFs realized, the last thing they should do is rush to live together, as it generally creates more problems than it solves. As self-directed SPSs, we're looking to shave off time to the altar, not slash our chances altogether.

In a culture contaminated by a poisonous "instant gratification" mind-set, people will often throw up their hands in resignation whenever a seemingly big obstacle comes along. When a couple is living together, in truth they have very little responsibility to each other, and hurdles like deciding who will clean the mountain of dirty dishes in the sink can seem like the Himalayas. People turn the small stuff into the insurmountable, eventually declaring insufferably, "I can't deal with this!" and checking out. Incidentally, even a blissful state of cohabitation while dating belies the challenges and hard work that sanctified marriage really embodies. Just as a race-car video game won't prepare you for your driver's test, living together while dating can never prepare you for marriage.

The truth is that this so-called extra insurance will never answer the questions you're hoping it will. That comes only with a lifetime of marriage behind you—you can't know how another person will react to situations that haven't even happened yet. And at what point is "enough time" enough? "I just want to see the way she handles this situation, and that one . . ." the PFs always say. But you can't possibly experience every permutation of every possible future event. It's a logic that's shortsighted and myopic at best. And at worst, it can sever an otherwise healthy relationship that was heading to the altar.

Like it or not, statistics do show a disproportionate divorce rate among those couples who lived together before tying the knot. Researchers in family studies routinely produce the same evidence, study after study: married couples who lived together before marriage are up to 50 percent more likely to divorce, citing poor communication, less conflict resolution, and weakness in spousal supportiveness. It's just the grim face of cohabitating reality—I don't make this stuff up.

If you don't know each other well enough—and you think living together will bridge that gap—then you shouldn't be getting married at all! And if your relationship is dotted with such doubt, then take the time to figure things out; playing house together without any shared responsibility will not fill in any of those gaps in a real, definitive way and can throw you off the marital course altogether.

The Common-Law Marriage Argument

In suggesting alternatives to an engagement, he lamely and oh-so-characteristically points out that your situation is basically common law anyway, so why do you need a marriage license? "Um, because this isn't 1066 medieval England and I'm not comfortable with your family deridingly calling me your concubine?" The only appropriate response to this question is: Sorry, Sir William of Indecision, I'm from a modernized country—the only real superpower, which has paved the way for novelties like Cheeto-flavored lip gloss—and I'd like to have this union recognized in the real world. Flavored lip glosses and a marriage license—is that too much to ask for in our short time on this earth?

Sure, the world has a few darlings of common law, like Susan Sarandon and Tim Robbins, but comparing yourself to celebrities is never a good idea. And anyway, besides cranking up the bright bulbs of noncommitment on the world's stage, do they seem especially happy except when they're Bush-bashing together?

Succumbing to his sheepish demands on this front is granting him extreme latitude and translates into zero accountability on his part. You'll be slipping through the technical cracks when the going gets tough, or when the tough start cheating (or whatever behavior he thinks he can get away with through this arrangement). If he's playing the

Common Law Marriage card, he's an abject emotional coward who can't summon the courage to be honest with himself or you or fully commit to the relationship.

How to Put Your Foot Down

There are ways to actually put your foot down without also putting it in your mouth. For instance, Savannah, twenty-seven, was never keen on the idea of living with someone before marriage. When her boyfriend of three years, Alan, suggested they get an apartment together in downtown Atlanta, she was very direct about her misgivings. "I wanted to live with him," she explained to me, "but I just didn't trust the idea without a real commitment from him. I told him that I would live with him only if we were engaged. He looked a little shocked at first but could tell I was serious." Three months later, Alan proposed, and Savannah happily packed her things. They moved in just a month before the wedding and have now been married for a year. "Moving in with him was tough! It definitely took some getting used to, and we had our share of arguments in the beginning as we got used to sharing space. I'm so glad I held out and that I had the ring to remind us both that we were in it for the long haul, and willing to do the work. Otherwise, he might have run for the hills!"

It's understandably hard to stand your ground, but you can still avoid a major blowup—if you get your PF to see *your* way of thinking, instead of acquiescing to his. You don't want to give in to him against your principles, but you don't want to lose him either, and you should tell him so. If he says he feels uncomfortable or unsure about marriage before moving in, remind him that commitment brings comfort—not the

other way around. Simply knowing you're in a sanctified relationship brings about a comfort level that no amount of
time living together unwed ever can. When you do have "the
talk" with him, lovingly reassure him that you have the ut-
most trust both in him and in your relationship, that nothing
will shake that trust, and that you don't think living together
is necessary to test the trust or compatibility between you.
Now how can he argue with that?

In the end, remember that if he insists on moving in—or
indicates that he absolutely will not consider an engagement
without a "test-drive"—you may just have to move on. He's
telegraphing to you with a bullhorn that he's not prepared to
marry you—but he is prepared to put you through an open-
ended trial. Instead of assembling your foolproof evidence,
forfeit your case altogether. The trial will never accomplish
what he thinks it will. If he needs so much convincing to take
this step, it's one he obviously isn't ready to take.

13

Strategy #4: Master the Art of Guilt-Free Manipulation

War is just when it is necessary; arms are permissible
when there is no hope except in arms.
—NICCOLO MACHIAVELLI

So your courtship is plodding along. Ten perfectly pleasant months have passed, but nothing seismic has occurred to bring the relationship to that next level, that watershed moment, the planting of the "this-could-be-the-one" seed in his head and the "wife" flag on your back. What to do?

Is he a rag doll? A piece of spineless clay to be molded? An impassive cold fish whose hard edges are in desperate need of softening? Yes, yes, and yes, respectively. Even if we often feel as though men are in the control room, there are some surefire techniques that you can employ to outfox the inferior gender and inspire in him a longing for marriage. Moralistic misgivings should be checked at the door for this chapter—if you want to make it down the aisle, your relationship needs directing and you're just the woman to do it.

This chapter will show you how to win over his closest confidants—family and friends; how to Flo Nightingale the hell out of him when he's sick; how to subtly induce a proposal; and how to avoid conniving too much and botching the whole relationship.

TACTIC #1: Get Him to Show Vulnerability

This strategy is a high-wire act of emotional duplicity, but simply look into your closetful of heinous bridesmaid taffeta and crinoline for inspiration, you moral acrobat. Ideally, you'll want to "accidentally" precipitate the discussion. Of course you'll have to dig for some deep-buried skeletons—some unpleasant experience buried in the dustbin of his past, preferably some episode ripped from those awkward middle school days of pubescent transition and gym locker room apprehensions. The goal is not to vitiate the poor recovering fencing camp nerd, but to empower him through your new brand of therapy.

Did he have a tough time adjusting to a new school? Were the only clothes he had in the New World those with Soviet stars still sewn into them? Is the torment of bullies still haunting him to the point that he sleeps with the light on? Without emasculating him, you want to get him to confide in you through sharing these rash-inducing memories—knowing that you still think he's the best thing since sliced matzo and even find his geekdom charming will engender trust and help seal the deal.

Example:

A former PF of mine seemed especially off one day. Now if I'd given him a penny for his thoughts every time he looked like he was contemplating something weighty, he wouldn't have been able to buy himself a day-old piece of bread. He lived his life flush on the surface and I loved him for it. But this time, I was determined to extract from him what was on his mind.

"It's really bad, it's about my family," he admitted.

"Oh, no, what happened?" I asked with frighteningly on-point alarm.

"They were forced to sell our house in the Hamptons!" he said, barely able to look me in the eye.

"Oh, no! I had no idea . . . is there anything I can do?" I asked, hoping to abate his crushing despair.

"Well, it's only half the house, really. But it's still really bad; now we have to share the backyard with strangers!"

Now, clearly this was not a crisis on par with world hunger or even my Aunt Sydney's recent onset of diabetes. But the point is that at that moment, my PF was hurting—on the shallow end of the pool, but still hurting—and I stepped in to offer support. It was my empathy that day that brought me that much closer to sharing said half of that Hamptons property. My PF responded to my compassion by increasingly opening up to me about his personal issues, becoming more openly demonstrative and emotionally attached. He came to realize that my unwavering support was the elusive quality he'd want in a wife and even started hinting about marriage. Of course by that point I realized spending my life with a social climber as shallow as he was could never afford me the kind of life I wanted, but the fundamental principles of supportiveness remain.

Quick Tip: Avoid Bruising His Fragile Ego by Clocking Him Where It Hurts

It's a beautiful spring day in New York; you're cavorting in Central Park with your PF, where the only noises you hear are the cries of Upper East Side children begging their parents to crush their Ritalin into ice cream instead of applesauce. Should you pass the Mr. Softee ice-cream truck, resist the urge to ask him if that was his high school nickname, even if you are only joking. This will more likely send him to therapy than into your arms; while you may think that prodding about something personal is the best way to get him to open up, it must be done with sensitivity. If you sense a vulnerability, approach with caution rather than catching him off guard.

For example, if you know his parents got divorced when he was four, instead of launching into a strident "Wow, that must have sucked! Do you think that screwed with your psychological balance?" tread softly and ask, "How was that growing up for you? That must have been so hard to go through at such a young age." Over time, he'll grow increasingly comfortable opening up to you with his emotions.

TACTIC #2: Win Over His Closest Confidants

We know you want to keep your PF at least six stripper pole lengths away from his recovering frat-boy friends who nourish the commitment-phobe pandemic, but you *must*, however, penetrate their domain at some point in order to get them to endorse you as a wife. Winning over two people— the best friend and then his nana—is more vital than ingratiating yourself with anyone else in his life. And if his nana's dead, you'll need to improvise and convince him you're channeling her spirit from beyond the grave. Bonus points if you convince him of a mystic miracle—that she has reappeared in order to tell her grandson to marry you, fast!

Whether you click or clash with these figures will dictate your marital fate. Getting in his friends' good graces carries with it the crucial vote of approval your impressionable PF needs to make a decision. His friends are just like yours (except they're trusted allies, not cutthroat competitors) and most likely they'll be too distracted by the playoffs or the finals or whatever's on TV to ever pierce your layers of deceit. This, after all, is still the set that's only recently replaced crushing empty beer cans against their heads with whipping out their Sidekicks. Remember, if they don't emphatically approve of you, they can poison the waters irreversibly.

This essential task is your black-diamond ski trail of manipulation. You may have a bunny slope mentality, but you'll need to up the ante on this one.

Five No-Fail Ways to Seamlessly Ingratiate Yourself with His Friends

1. You track down Craig from Craigslist himself in a valiant effort to score tickets to the World Cup match your PF's best friend has been talking about endlessly. (Use your connections at *Sports Illustrated* to get Pedro to meet him personally and start practicing your loudest "SCOOOOORE!!!!")

2. Did one of his frat-boy friends manage to get himself fired from—of all things—a union job? Now's the time to call in a favor to your uncle, the HR director at a major communications firm, and get the self-professed "people person" an interview at the company.

3. You're a hit at the dinner party you throw for his boorish buddies while your PF's out of town on business. You're a veritable cultural chameleon, prodigiously laughing at every lowbrow attempt at a joke and smiling through every refill of their imported beer.

4. Pretend to be that empathetic ear, affecting your best "concern" for their mind-numbing issues ("I banged her two days ago—do you think I should call her tomorrow or Thursday?").

5. Assure them that you have lots of attractive female friends—thereby insinuating that if there's a wedding, there will be hot girls aplenty in the hotel banquet hall, where the proximity to their overnight pad will really work in their favor!

Five No-Fail Ways to Get in—and Stay in—His Family's Good Graces

While his friends carry plenty of weight in your PF's dating decisions, his family's role cannot be underestimated. Cozy up to them by whatever means necessary; it may not be your finest hour, but for the sake of your nuptials, this is a must-do. This is your chance to get in good with his nana, his sister, even the family dog! Tips to getting in good:

1. Invite Nana to a knitting class at the nouveau chic yarn shop on your block. Her heyday ended long before the war, so she'll likely be thrilled with the attention. It'll keep her occupied—and in your corner—for a while.

2. Massaging his dog and his nana are not altogether different: both are cute, cuddly, and don't say much—but when they approve of you, he'll know it. Buy a couture-cute dog sweater for Sammy and present it in time for the first November chill.

3. If you know his sister just broke into the world of academia at a local community college, clip that recent

article from the paper about the national spike in community college enrollment. She'll genuinely appreciate the interest you've taken in her life and it's that thoughtfulness that's key in clinching the family endorsement.

4. Never miss an opportunity to pitch in with the dishes at the family home. Your dishpan hands may require an extra manicure, but no mother can resist the idea of a good-natured team player taking care of her favorite son.

5. Show up. Just getting face time at major family milestones—like his parents' thirtieth wedding anniversary or their annual family softball game—will leave a huge imprint and show that you are in it for the long haul.

Always do your best to mask your devious motives. All the heavy lifting now will be well worth it once you get their vote, but with a group that's constantly scrutinizing you, you can't be sloppy at this stage of the game.

TACTIC #3: Employ the "Dying Grandparent" Technique

When Emily, twenty-nine, came back empty handed from a carefully timed romantic trip to the Bahamas with her PF of two years, her friends' reactions confirmed what she had to do. When she returned with only a sunburn and a boyfriend rather than a fiancé, their disappointment was obvious. "I think one of them lost fifty bucks on a bet. One good friend said, 'Oh, I feel so sad for you that you came up short this week. What is Michael waiting for? Another romantic vacation that would be a perfect place to do it?!' " Emily recalls with disgust.

But that friend's expression of disappointment was exactly what she needed to spring into action. And action she took. "After that point, my mission was to get him to pro-pose—fast!" she recalls. All her heavy-handed hinting had gone only so far toward whipping her PF into shape. But she knew there was one last no-fail trick up her sleeve: the old "dying grandparent" ploy. Here's how it works:

- Explain to your PF that there's nothing more mean-ingful to you than having your grandparents alive to see the wedding.
- Explain what a big blow it would be to have a beloved family member miss out on the wedding by a matter of a mere months and how devastated you would be if he did nothing to prevent that.
- Keep addressing your grandpa as "Colonel," and salute him every time he walks into the room. He'll look naturally bewildered, scratching his head earnestly; make sure your PF is there to witness just how "feeble" Grandpa is becoming.
- Emphasize how it was always your grandma's dream to see you at your wedding, so unless he wants to deny a dying woman her final wish . . . (you should also remind him that she has a will that would most certainly include a new grandson in the family).

After her next vacation, five months later, Emily and her friends were sated with a prize cut of an engagement ring. As a last resort, it really works.

TACTIC #4: Flo Nightingale the Hell out of Him When He's Sick
Florence Nightingale, bless her uncontaminated heart, was a nurse in nineteenth-century Italy with all the right intentions and, as history's raised curtain reveals, all the right seductive

charms. Her ministrations would raise the spirits and appendages of her ailing male patients, who would regularly fall in love with the woman who brought them back to life, emotionally and physically. This is where the similarities between you and Flo end, because she—and if you're faint of heart, close your eyes now—declined a proposal from the highly prominent English politician Richard Monckton Milnes, because, of all things, she thought marriage would interfere with nursing.

Take it from me: there's no feeling a woman can experience—except possibly for childbirth or watching that annoying friend who's never single pack on ten pounds—that evokes as much pleasure and pure joy as taking care of her ailing PF and using her nurturing magic to nurse him back to health. Watching him bask gratefully in your care really is a thing of beauty. But you can't always rely on Mother Nature to unleash her medical wrath on your PF. What if the little troublemaker works out four times a week? Does yoga? Eats kale?! Not to worry, there are still plenty of opportunities to show off your caretaking capabilities.

Maggie, twenty-five, insists the proof is in the proposal. She hadn't even heard of the enterprising Nurse Flo when she dutifully tended to her PF, who had suffered a serious sports injury—but she sure is grateful for the Flo Effect now that she is engaged. "Anthony was homebound for two weeks and I was on call 24/7, but despite him not being in the best spirits while I was at his beck and call, the experience somehow fused us together." Three weeks later Anthony proposed—a move whose catalyst seemed clear. After little more than a year of dating, Maggie never saw it coming, but attributes his shift in momentum to her well-intentioned nursing. "I think that experience simply made him see me in a very new light—as someone who would always take care of him and not complain about it, no matter what."

So the next time your man gets a lashing from Mother Nature's whip—even a Sunday-morning hangover will do—bust out your best Flo Nightingale impression. You're not looking for a Golden Lamp Award here, just a ring, so don't fret too much over your true ability to heal. All you need to be concerned with is being attentive and stocking up on his favorite comfort foods—and you'll make a believer out of your PF in no time.

Whatever it is that knocks him off balance is your perfect opportunity to nurse that kvetching baby back to health. There are lots of moments to look forward to: flu season is never far away, offices are always over-air-conditioned during the summer, not to mention all the germ-laden gym equipment he regularly uses, so there should be no shortage of opportunities to swoop in and save the day with your thoughtfulness.

Does he have a particular skin allergy you gleaned from swiped medical records? If you notice he's looking a little splotchy lately, accompany him the next time he does laundry—also a great way to display your domestic heart of gold!—and point out how his detergent is irritating his delicate skin. You'll be slathering cream on him for days *and* be the hero for sparing a bad skin reaction in the future! Don't think of this as making a Faustian deal with Doree. You're not necessarily manipulating this unfortunate health situation, you're simply milking it for all it's worth—a huge legal difference, trust me.

When he's sick with that inevitable winter cold, you can *slowly*—just to make sure he knows how much he owes his life to you (wink, wink)—and tenderly nurse him back to health. Look your imperiled PF in the eye lovingly, and reassure him that you'll always be there to take care of him. He'll be so grateful for the gift of your care that he'll (re)discover how important you are to him—too important to let go.

Here are just a few strategies for showcasing your nurturing side:

- If he's complaining of a sore throat, leave him apple slices with honey and a note wishing him a "sweet day."
- If he's so bleary-eyed that he can't distinguish week-old shrimp salad in the back of the fridge from the milk, be sure to intercept the dicey move and save him from a gastronomic close call.
- If it seems like he's having a rough day, get the recipe for his favorite fudge brownies from his mom and make them, or at least learn the location of the closest bakery that can.
- Not too pricey, with a big payoff: if he's off work for the week, surprise him with Movies on Demand. Your thoughtfulness and generosity will not be forgotten!

Manipulations That May Backfire

Kendall, thirty-one, is concerned that women can irreversibly tear the fabric of their relationships through scheming. She insists that guys like her own fiancé do not like to be manipulated. So what's your point, Kendall? We disembarked from that port a while ago, honey! The tactics in this chapter take for granted that your relationship isn't made of cheap fabric

anyway—they assume that you and your PF really are meant
to be, he just needs a little nudging along the way. That said,
the following examples might be taking premarital manipulation and trickery just a little too far:

- Don't let him find out that you're engaged by having
  the coordinator at the catering hall you've already
  booked for next June call him to confirm his credit
  card number.
- Don't have the minister surprise him one day in ser-
  vices by announcing your engagement in front of the
  whole congregation, stunning everyone, particularly
  him.
- Don't secretly sign you both up for the "How to Buy
  the Perfect Diamond" class at Tiffany's. Price: twenty-
  five dollars per person, half price if scorned SPS
  brings her inconsolable mother for moral support
  when PF dumps her on the spot.
- Don't fake a pregnancy. This is an all-or-nothing
  deal, and if you test your manipulation skills on this
  tightrope of a scheme, you are asking for big, big
  trouble.

I had a onetime friend—God bless her corroded heart,
but she was way too panicked even for me—who was so focused on getting married that she persuaded her feeble-
spined boyfriend to open a "ring fund." You know—a fund
by which money is funneled from, say, a PF's retirement fund
of tomorrow or the electricity bill of last week into a non-
interest-bearing account for her future engagement bling. Yes,
this poor guy was more or less caught in the grip of a very,
um, authoritative girlfriend. That is, until he finally found the
pants she stole from him and started to wear them in this re-

lationship again. He realized that her antics had finally gone too far and—upon counsel from his friends and family—decided to leave her. Remember: those tenuous morals that you used to be so proud of *do* have their consequences. So if any tactic you employ makes you feel uncomfortable deep down, pay attention and abort the mission; exfoliating twice a week and destroying all evidence of the loofah still won't take care of that nagging feeling that you just might have plotted yourself right out of the party.

Ultimately, you don't want to conscript a man who becomes your husband just because you wore him down. Okay, well maybe you do right now, but if you look at this situation with some perspective, you might change your mind. In the hinterlands of your heart, you know squeezing a proposal out of him under these conditions isn't what's going to make you happy. "You can push all you want, but ultimately it's his decision," reinforces that persistent SAP Kendall. "And all of your nagging and pushing won't force him to do anything he doesn't want to do."

14

Strategy #5: Learn How to Counter Classic Smoke Screens

He may be trying every trick he's got up his sleeve to throw you off the wedding trail, but that ain't gonna repel you! Your PF better find a new bag of tricks. You're determined to stay the course and you're going to wear him down and get him to marry you whether he likes it or not. Remember the Bonnie Raitt song "I Can't Make You Love Me"? Wanna bet?

This chapter will teach you how to counter the top five excuses that PFs use to delay marriage proposals; assess any signs of straying or jealousy—and what they say about the durability of your relationship; and avoid succumbing to marital martyrdom by proposing to him.

The Top Five Excuses for Not Getting Married

1. He says, "I never grew up with love, I don't know how to love."

What's the deal? Sure, your PF may genuinely feel disillusioned toward matrimony, proclaiming a miracle any time he sees a happily married couple. Haunted by his parents' divorce, perhaps he can't shake his jaundiced views toward marriage or relationships. While he may have real issues with trust and closeness, it's no reason for him to shut you—or the idea of marriage—out completely.

How to counter it: Reassure him that he is his own person who needn't repeat the mistakes of any family members from the past. Remind him that you two write your own ticket together—you're building your lives from a solid place and nothing will change that. If he continues to tell himself that he can never find and keep true happiness with a woman, then he won't. But if he makes an effort to dismiss those inner demons, there's no reason he can't cultivate a deep, committed relationship with you.

2. He proclaims, "I refuse to get married before the state of Michigan recognizes gay marriage!"

What's the deal? His legitimate grievance with the justice system may be one of the things you most admire about him. You respect his crusade to give everyone a voice—but now all you want to do is muzzle his. "Does he have to take a moral stand at the expense of our future?" you think—and rightfully so. Well, you picked this liberal humanitarian to love, and now you're going to have to deal with the consequences.

How to counter it: Brad Pitt may be able to get away with this excuse, but look at him—he's Brad Pitt, he can do whatever he wants! Your PF, on the other hand, should not get a pass that easily. If you want to get him off his moral high horse and get married, tell him that although you love his passion, he should save his boycott for a public forum, not your personal relationship. And while his conviction is something you admire, he can't stand up for everyone else's rights while ignoring his girlfriend's needs altogether.

3. "I lived half my life in the USSR, under the thumb of a dictatorial, corrupt Communist government. I don't like authority telling me what to do and I'm not capitulating to societal standards again!"

What's the deal? As his girlfriend of three years, all you can say is "Thanks, Stalin, you piece of shit, for sabotaging my dream of marriage!" Your scarred PF bears understandable resentment toward the establishment—any establishment, really—for encroaching on every aspect of people's lives and now overcompensates in every area in order to assert his autonomy over his own life.

How to counter it: Just because he's a nontraditionalist doesn't mean he shouldn't try to make you happy if a conventional marriage is what you want. Tell him that while it is a regulated institution, your union isn't on anyone else's terms—it's on yours and yours alone. Plus, applying for a marriage license is nothing like waiting in a bread line.

4. "You never told me you wear hair extensions! How can I trust you in a marriage if I can't trust you with this?"

What's the deal? Upon finding ribbons of nylon extensions socked away in your underwear drawer—which suddenly makes your padded push-up bras less of a transgression—he grows suspicious of you and starts to question the trust in your relationship.

How to counter it: While he may think something like this shouldn't have been covered up, more than likely he is just using it as an excuse to drive a wedge between you. If he's trying the "if it's hair extensions today, what will it be tomorrow?" logic, don't fall for it. Sure, a lie is a lie, but he's definitely working with ulterior motives here. I've never known a solid couple to part ways over nylon anything, so if he is indeed just looking for an excuse to bolt, send this cowardly PF packing.

5. "It's good luck to get married in the Year of the Dog."

What's the deal? Your conversation with your PF goes something like this:

> PF: "But I'd really feel better if we could get married in a good luck year—I heard it's the Year of the Dog."
> YOU: "According to whom?"
> PF: "Chinese proverbs dating back thousands of years—that's good enough for me."
> YOU: "But you're Irish . . . and you don't even believe in fortune cookies. Well, okay, but when is the next Year of the Dog?"
> PF: "2018—but it'll be so worth it, baby!"

Talk about the year of the dog. His superstitions might run deep, but your patience does not (2018—is he kidding?!). If you know your PF to be a horseshoe-wearing, rabbit's-foot-clasping, four-leaf-clover-loving believer, then this excuse might be legit, if still extreme. But if this interest in superstition seems to be coming out of nowhere, it may be a poorly disguised stall tactic.

How to counter it: Tell your PF that your relationship transcends luck and superstitious symbols. If your love is real, then you don't need "luck" from an outside force—everything you need for a successful relationship is already within your grasp.

So He's Trying to Cut You Loose

We've all been there. He says he's ending it. You pretend you're impervious. He gets a restraining order. You send it through the paper shredder. It's a contest of wills, you're thinking, and you don't want to be the last unmarried standing. But no one wants to be that SPS who's willing to settle for crumbs, insisting on milking the relationship like a tube of toothpaste on its last leg—wringing it for that last bit, choking what little life it has left. Your old motto, "No one unilaterally walks away from a relationship with me and still has his kneecaps to show for it," isn't the best mantra for a girl with self-respect and a mature outlook on life and love.

In all seriousness, some PFs can genuinely get cold feet about getting married. And while a certain degree of doubt on his end is normal and shouldn't be cause for alarm, sometimes the signs are just too blatant to ignore. If you can't shake the feeling that he wants to run—for good—either confront him about his wayward behavior or take the cue and get out of the sinking relationship. Not even the most desperate SPS should waste her time with a PF who will never pop the question.

Signs he might be straying:

- He says he's committed to that Jews for Jesus thing, and doesn't have time to see you because he has to hand out literature again this weekend.
- He stops payment on the check to the premarital therapist you've been seeing.
- He cancels your weekend plans at the beach, claiming that he has to do his taxes. Even though it's July.
- He says he's coming down with a bad case of small-pox. "Really?" you say in your best clipped voice. "The disease that's been eradicated for a century?!"

The fact is, only you know how your PF acts in your relationship. If you genuinely sense that his behavior has been off—for no external reason—then you'll need to figure out an appropriate way to confront the situation. If you're especially attuned to your PF, then detecting unusual behavior won't be hard. Canceling plans without being especially apologetic, making excuses to avoid spending time together, and emotionally or physically withdrawing are never good signs. But burying your head in the sand and praying he snaps out of it won't bring you any closer to a resolution. You need to address these changes you're noticing with your guy—without grilling him like an attack dog, but not taking any guff either—if you want to get your relationship back on track.

How to Pull Him Back In—or, If Need Be, Send Him Back to the Fishes

The bottom line is, you can't leave your future happiness to chance. He might be harboring genuine concerns about moving forward and these issues might be easily resolved—but not without patiently talking to him about his feelings of uneasiness.

Sure, the changes in your relationship might seem as inexplicable as Ryan Seacrest's rise to fame, but once you directly address them, any ambiguity will likely be cleared up; if he stammers and indelicately switches subjects, there may be trouble. But chances are, he has good reason for his uncharacteristic behavior—and it might not have anything to do with you. You cannot presume to know what's in his head or his heart without talking to him calmly and openly; more often than not, a quick, straightforward talk will clear up any mixed signals you may be receiving. Of course if he's leaving you with a trail of clues that allow you no other conclusion except that he wants out of the relationship for good, then gladly send this lemon back where it belongs. If he's too cowardly to break up with you directly and instead starts forcing you away, then save him the time and trouble and end it yourself—and move on to a prospect who isn't wearing his bridal-proof vest.

Your Own Jealousy: Natural or Cause for True Alarm?

A small dose of jealousy is never a bad thing. Your exhibition of minor jealousy reminds your PF that you're protective of him—that you have tentacles and know how to use them—and that you love him. Besides, most men like to see their women get territorial now and then. But if you're feeling jealous on a regular basis, you have to ask yourself if there may be something more to your PF's behavior. Is he genuinely starting to engage with other women in a way that suggests he's no longer fully invested in your relationship—and may be planning an exit strategy? Or is he merely clinging to the last shreds of his bachelorhood because he knows the end— as well as the wedding—is just around the corner?

Whenever there was an attractive girl on the periphery, my past PF's eyes would dart back and forth so often they looked like Ping-Pong balls. There were other questionable comments that gave me clues: "I can't understand why cheating isn't accepted in today's culture. Fifty years ago the wife would turn the other cheek," he'd pontificate. "Since it usually means nothing anyway, what's the harm in it?" If this PF wasn't telegraphing his intention to cheat, he was certainly defending his rationalization of it. And either way, no one needs a catch of the day like that, as voracious as one might be. So you must ask yourself: is your jealousy unfounded? What's the root of it? And are you prepared to carry it with you forever?

For those who've experienced firsthand how cheating decimates a marriage (either your parents' or Charlie Sheen's), there is certainly valid concern that it could be echoed in your own relationship. But if it's more than that, if you feel more than passing pangs of jealousy when you see your PF noticing another woman, your instincts might be fighting to tell you something your head's trying to dismiss. Here are some warning signs to consider:

- Is he actually giving you reasons to be jealous? Does he try to make you jealous beyond a fun, lighthearted tease?
- Have you discovered anything zebra-printed in his underwear drawer, especially when he knows you're allergic to crudely made animal-print undies?
- Does he often measure you against the meter stick of

past girlfriends, reinforcing the fact that you might come up short?

• Is the aforementioned zebra-printed unmentionable in thong form?

The bottom line: if his heartless pronouncements and heavy-handed messages seem like more than your standard case of proposal impotence, then his wandering eye can serve as a blessing in disguise to start rethinking the durability of this relationship. If you do find yourself negotiating your inner demons, feeling unsure and nervous about him straying and where you stand, you must determine if this is just a hologram in your head. A gaping lack of trust on your side, or on his, means you both need to do some major introspection and trace its root. If you're entering into a marriage with even the slightest doubt about whether his interest in other women may really manifest itself, make sure it's just paranoia, not perceptiveness.

Marital Martyrdom: Should You Ever Cave and Propose to Him?

Should you ever check your pride at the door and just ask him? Should any SPS at the end of her rope take charge of the situation and turn her Kafkaesque haze into a clear reality?

In my impressionable teen days, I remember watching a banner being unfurled across my town's main drag, reading, "Kenny, will you marry me?" I don't know whatever happened to Kenny, but I have a pretty good idea of how his girlfriend's love life devolved. What made this poor, misguided gender bender think that postmodern murkiness can cloud gender roles to this extreme? It's the old matrimonial car wreck—too gory to watch, yet you can't turn away. I know it's the twenty-first century and women can make overtures on dates, in the bedroom, and in tax fraud undertakings, but at least have some self-respect and dignity when it comes to popping the question! You aren't "taking one for the team" here—you're essentially destroying any team morale by stepping up and proposing yourself. Remember, to hear that resounding "Yes!" is the stuff of marital manipulators' dreams. To hear sirens at your door ready to haul you off to the loony bin is the stuff of reality.

Still in doubt? Let's look at the facts. Check out the ill-fated attempts of marital masochists to supplant the man in his time-honored role:

- Britney popped the question to K-Fed and popped a few blood vessels after the divorce filing two years later. Even her kabbalah bracelet couldn't save her from the disaster that unfolded after she bought her own diamond!
- Pink got down on bended neon and proposed to her husband. But with that tough-as-nails image that could make Attila the Hun quake, anyone could predict her suitor would buckle and accept so as not to unleash her unrequited wrath.
- Lorelai Gilmore, the smart-mouthed mom, proposed to Luke on *Gilmore Girls,* only to break off the engagement right before showtime.
- Miranda on *Sex and the City* made an impromptu proposal to Steve, but at least she could fall back on the cheap beer she was gulping by the gallon at the time as an excuse.

A Proposal Fit for a Queen

While in most cases proposing to him is as good as checking your pride and semisoiled reputation at the door, there is one precedent that didn't end too badly. Already a queen in 1839, Victoria made royal waves by proposing to her underage cousin Prince Albert. The queen may have buckled in proposing, but they did lead a very rich life together—financially and spiritually.

But for the rest of us, holding court as the Queen of Panic is still better than holding court as the Queen of Shamelessness. Remember, you're far from royalty and you certainly don't have the pedigree or riches of a queen—so don't try this at home!

If you're about to pull the trigger and do something rash, ask yourself this: are you confident in the emphatic, overjoyed "Yes!" response? Of course you're not. That's why you've sunken to these depths. You're like Venice, but actualized in Cleveland. Face it, ladies: if he wanted to marry you, he would. Proposals from desperate SPSs are the stuff of which blogosphere humiliation is made. No one's denying this desperate move is good for a cheap laugh, but you'll be the only one not laughing when he freaks out. No one says you don't have guts—but more important than guts is pride.

Becca, single and twenty-seven, had something else to say on the matter: "I have a friend who's getting married soon, despite the fact that her fiancé has cheated on her repeatedly. Everyone seems to know this but her, and we were all hoping that she'd wise up and dump the jerk. But apparently, she said to him, 'If you don't ask me to marry you, I'll ask you to marry me.' And she did! And somehow, it worked and he said yes. But the primary point I'm trying to make here is that if she wanted to get married and he wasn't asking, she should have taken it as a sign and moved on."

Becca's story underscores just how vital it is that the man propose. To set the tone of a marriage knowing that your intended was the passive recipient of a proposal can't be the most auspicious start to a union. If your PF isn't asking, you can be assured there's a reason why. And it just might be that you're better off without him.

So no matter how desperate and impatient you feel, hold off on getting down on bended knee at all costs. Let him rise to your level, don't lower yourself to his; if he wants to marry you, he will make it happen. And while some typical dating smoke screens are easy to see through—and are usually just your average case of preproposal jitters—if the signs that he's not ready and wants out of the relationship are glaring, do yourself a favor and move on.

15

Strategy #6: Creep into His Subconscious— and Stay There

Trespassing into his mind is a fail-safe way of manipulating him without any messy fingerprints. Before you can say "black tie optional," you have planted the message "you = woman of his dreams = wedding." The importance of planting subliminal messages cannot be overstated—this can very well serve as his crucial nuptial tailwind. It's not so much the intellectual decisions your PF will be making that determine if you're The One, it's the feelings behind the intellectualization, the subconscious nudgings behind the methodical decision making. In that vein, you want to do everything in your power to hijack his subconscious and plant the seeds that will propel him toward marriage.

In this chapter, you will learn how to get inside your PF's mind and covertly spread your seeds into his psyche; determine what may be holding him back; and plant the positive reinforcement your relationship needs. You will also find out how to respond if, after chipping away at his male brain, you don't like what you see after all.

How to Spread Your Wedding Seeds—Surreptitiously

We'll get to spreading *those* seeds in a bit, but for right now, it's crucial to plant the wedding seeds in his head, knowing you're on fertile ground. Remember to let *him* arrive at the idea of getting married. Mounting "your case" can translate into him feeling forced into it—flattening your long-held wedding plans. But if he thinks he's the initiator, it will psychologically sit much more soundly with him—and make him that much more inclined to make your dreams of marriage actionable.

While dating one PF, I tactically executed all the right moves, checked off all the appropriate benchmarks at their appropriate times—to the point where there was such a level of comfort on his end that there was nothing left for him to do but propose. And after months of blueprints and tactical briefings, it finally paid off. The moment I'd waited for with baited breath since the ugliest girl in my high school class got engaged at last came to fruition; the magic words I'd been waiting for him to say finally saw the light of day: "Doree," he said, looking deeply into my eyes, "you're ready to be married." I exulted, my heart filled with helium—but only to myself . . . and only for three seconds: "You're ready to be married to someone who will appreciate how special you are." Huh? I don't know which was worse: being excused from a relationship because I was ready to be married and he wasn't or having him say the complete opposite of what I'd hoped. But to be sure, a woman's choices are never easy. Apparently, my hints at marriage were about as subtle as a Don Imus jab.

Attacking him or pointedly pushing an agenda will only make him defensive and—subconsciously or not—inevitably force him to push you away. So, if you know your PF to be pigheaded—and telling him to go right will automatically make him go left—you'll have to resort to subtler tactics to effect your desired results.

Technique #1: Put Your Words into Someone Else's Mouth—Get Your Friends to Talk About Weddings

If you know that berating him about your missing hand hardware will only cause him to dig his feet in, then make sure he overhears the argument from someone else. Hearing those pro-marriage talking points from your mutual married friends Tom and Susie won't put him on the defensive as it would hearing them directly from you, and he'll be able to absorb the message rather than immediately rejecting it. In other words, see to it that you're in social situations in which pro-marriage conversations will flow freely. Keeping company with happy, stable couples is a great way to make this happen.

When infiltrating his inner psychological sanctum, the roundabout route will always be much more effective than the direct offensive—especially when it comes to marriage talk. Making sure he overhears his best friend saying he's afraid to lose his much-loved girlfriend if he doesn't hold on to her tightly enough will get your own PF thinking that much more critically about his own chances of losing you if he doesn't make a major effort to step it up.

Technique #2: Gently Seep into His Subconscious, Then His Dreams

Any psychologist you ask will attest to the unlimited power of the subconscious and of the mind's suggestibility while in sleeping or dreaming states. Try talking to him on the phone right before he drifts off to sleep. If you're the last person he thinks about before bed, you will gently seep into his subconscious and then into his dreams, transmitting your bridal brainwaves. Purposely hang up the phone—whoops! dropped call—during a pivotal, soul-fusing moment, in which he is longing for emotional connection and satisfaction. The more he thinks about you when he's drifting off to sleep, the more deeply your life will be intertwined with his.

Technique #3: Send the Right Subliminal Messages

Work the words *wedding* and *marriage* into your conversations as often as possible. And make sure that the broader concept of marriage enters his sphere as well. Keep in mind, however, that watching Colin Cowie shows together is good, watching episodes of *Bridezillas* is not. The images evoked should be pleasant and safe, not ones that could be registered as threatening. It's a big plus if you two are at dinner and you've arranged for a plant to gush, "Oh, you two are so cute, are you engaged?" "Oh, thank you!" you'll shyly answer her. "No, we're not, but it is only 7:30." If the idea of marriage is in his head, then it will eventually pass down into his heart—where it's truly absorbed. When he sees everyone else consider you as that cute-as-a-button couple, it's tantamount to him starting to see it for himself too.

Subconscious Deal Breakers: What's Really Holding Him Back

Sure, a person isn't just a set of qualities, a pro/con list, and the whole is more than the sum of the parts. (But are you sure your PF knows that?) But deep inside that mind of his, your PF is subconsciously tallying all your moves—especially the ones in the bedroom and the kitchen. Therefore, in addition to the techniques you're trying on him, subtle behavioral changes—simple, yet seismic measures—on your part can make the crucial difference in his subconscious.

Problem #1: He Views Your Cluttered House as the Sign of a Cluttered Life

The lights are low, you're clinging tightly to each other to generate some heat amid this winter's harshness, and you're testing your couch cushions' durability while the two of you "watch a movie." And when he goes in deep, he comes out with . . . that electric bill from December stuffed inside one of the cushions?? So that's where it was hiding! That explains why you've had "mood lighting" for three months and you've sported a consistent shade of blue—you've had no working heat or electricity!

SPS's delusion du jour: "But if he really loves me and wants to marry me, he won't let this domestic divide stop him."

Solution: Okay, so you're not the compulsive cleaning type, but have you been mistakenly inhaling any unused household products? Because you're suffering from the kind of delusion only serious ammonias could induce. The fact is that a failure to put your personal stamp on your home doesn't make much of a case for you in the homemaker department.

Shove every belonging that, if unearthed, would make him run screaming in the other direction into your closet with a thousand locks on it. That means every piece of unanswered mail (bonus points if you answer it!), every Learning Annex course catalog with the "Stop Procrastinating Now!" course flagged, every Twinkie wrapper you tore into with a friend's engagement party invitation, and that killer wedding gown you saw on sale for two hundred dollars three years ago that would have been criminal not to buy. If I had a dollar for every time I heard "Your apartment's a mess—how can you live like this?" I could have bought myself my own engagement ring by now!

I know, I know, you would clean your place if only that cleaning agent's opening weren't clogged with coagulation after years of non-usage. Honestly—who has time for tidying when panicking is a full-time job? But nevertheless, tidy up and show him that you know how to take care of yourself like an adult, and he will subconsciously see that you can take care of him too.

The ultimate sign of the homemaker? Start knitting. You know what, you don't even have to knit, just get yourself a knitting set, even if you can't thread an eye (or just had to run to ask someone what "threading an eye" means). It appears to inspire confidence in men. You're domestic, resourceful, you'll knit sweaters to keep him warm. The knitters on the bus and subway are always the ones with the wedding bands. Do the math!

Not the domestic diva type? Try looking centered when you're really on the fringes; always keep a yoga mat in plain sight. Let him think you're "Om"-ing your way to channeling your inner zen when you're really "Oh my God"-ing about not being married yet. Plus, Marc Jacobs has a really adorable yoga mat and matching tote that's to die for!

Moral of the story: channel your inner Betty Crocker—even if it kills you. Even if he doesn't say it outwardly, his subconscious says it all: in a wife, PFs are looking for a homemaker, a *balebusta* who can take over where their moms left off. (*Balebusta*, by the way, is Yiddish for eminent homemaker. And learn Yiddish! Never underestimate the power of knowing how to interject well-timed Yiddish phrases around the house.) So, next time you set off a mini-fire burning that cookie dough in yet another foray into fine cuisine, spin the situation by confessing that your love for him ignited those flames and nothing could extinguish them.

And, at the very least, prominently displaying a jar of Mrs. Dash seems to do the trick. After all, he doesn't need every meal to stick to his stomach if you really are a woman who feeds his soul. So don't think you have to reach Martha Stewart–like fanaticism. Any reheated processed dinner that looks authentic enough should help you clinch your engagement.

Problem #2: You're Not Snow White

How many notches do you have in your garter belt, and what does it say about you? You needn't be Snow White, but Sullied White just doesn't have the same ring to it either. Of course men, with their fragile egos, like to feel superior in the bedroom. Take for instance my last PF, who unbeknownst to me was looking for sanctity in a soul mate. Learning that I'd had any physical contact with other people was a completely off-putting concept for him, though he himself had sown his wild oats and realized the error of his ways years later. Therefore, his subconscious reservations about "us" lay squarely with my purity quotient—if we were to be married, he'd want an unquestionably "pure" wife to bless the new bed. This is the ultimate paradoxical quandary: most men want a consummate sexual partner, but one who is still a good girl.

SPS's delusion du jour: "He's never going to find out my real number of past sex partners, so why should I admit it and risk him getting permanently turned off and walking away?"

Solution: The truth always comes out—in one way or another—so I wouldn't suggest lying about your number to the man you want to marry. You never know when, after too many mojitos at dinner with the gang, a friend could inadvertently blab about your Spanish conquest in Ibiza last year, so being up front and honest with the person you're supposed to trust most is always the best solution. If you are at the serious stage in your relationship of discussing your sexual pasts—and by this point you should know each other very well!—then fudging your numbers shouldn't be necessary. He will accept whatever single—or even double-digit—number yours might be. Whatever it is, you won't scream "slut" in his head, but you may scream "trusting" and "foolish"—for having rushed into sexual relationships with guys who failed you. This is a perfect opportunity to reiterate why it's so important to you to wait to have sex until your relationship is planted on very solid ground.

Celibacy—it's the new black: Having sex too early in the relationship leaves your PF nothing to earn, nothing to work for, and with disproportionate leverage in the relationship. So

your ticket to overcoming the purity hurdle and keeping him
on his toes is to become a sex(less) goddess—learn to wrap
him around your little (reclaimed) hymen. You don't have to
actually wait until you're married, but if you're serious about
this PF, waiting just a little—coinciding with major milestones in your relationship, like vacations and lots of mutual
family time—really works.

If there's any chance that you can see yourself getting
more antsy that he won't call with the same frequency, or that
he'll start to pull away, then sex is entering the equation way
too soon. It should really come at a point when you feel so
confident in the relationship and in his intentions toward you
that it just feels right between you two without causing major
anxiety afterward. This could come at three months, or at
nine, as every couple's development progresses differently, but
you will know it when you have it.

Ariel, twenty-nine, got married last year. Bully for her.
"Even though I've had sex with boyfriends before, Joe and I
decided to wait until marriage so it would feel more special."
When Ariel confessed to Joe, "I don't want to have sex if we're
not going to stay together," his response reassured her that she
was with the right guy: "Why would we ever break up?"

Relationships heat up in two ways—microwaved or oven-
roasted. Both means achieve almost equal heat, but only one of
them sustains the relationship's longevity. Microwaves speed
things up, condensing steps and time. But just as quickly as the
microwaved item heats up, so too does it cool down with
equal speed. The oven-roasted relationships admittedly take
longer to achieve, but the main dish undeniably tastes much
better and stays warmed longer.

Of course it's about as unrealistic that you abstain from
sex with your PF as Rush Limbaugh will abstain from prescription pain killers. As a child how many times were you

caught with your hand in the condom jar? Hey, everyone's guilty here! But fueling this element of your relationship too soon can help to seal your relationship kiss of death.

So calm down your overeager beaver! This perceived sexual starvation isn't about playing games and cruelly withholding a key ingredient in a relationship's secret recipe (OK, maybe a little). Mostly it's about creating something that transcends the purely physical—and ensuring that your PF subconsciously recognizes that. It's the ultimate way to discover the deepest and richest layers of one another once you are *in* a committed relationship. While the physical aspect is crucial to any relationship, it's the emotional and intellectual elements that nurture the physical. Sex isn't the magic elixir to an ailing relationship; that's like trying to support a shaky bridge with a toothpick. So if you want your romance to go the distance, freeze the premature sex and let him warm up to you in a *real* way.

Ours is a sexually liberated culture—a culture of celebrity sex tapes as stocking stuffers and sluts-in-training starting bootylicious camp as young as age seven. And while it's highly improbable that any couple would commit to anything long-term without test-driving the goods before purchase—no one in his right mind would buy on the spot. Don't confuse sexual penetration with penetration of the soul if it's a ring you're after.

What to Do Once You've Gotten a Good Look Inside

You've tapped into his psyche—congratulations. But now that you've uncovered the machinations of his mind, you might not like what's been revealed. If his subconscious speaks as subtly as a bullhorn blasted in your ear that he might not share your vision for a loving, egalitarian marriage, it's time for some personal reevaluation. If your PF is any of the following "Ds," you might reconsider retiring that PF hunting rifle—since you might need it again sooner than you think.

Destructive: Is your PF sabotaging your relationship by refusing to accompany you to family functions or partake of regular activities—vacations, office parties, birthday celebrations—that couples normally do?

Distracted: His blank stare was kind of cute at first, but now his attention has been diverted for weeks. You don't get the feeling that he's truly focused on you or your relationship.

Disinterested: Does he constantly tell you that he has no space in his head for your "trivial" problems? When you have an agonizing monthlong feud with your sister, does he make it clear that he just doesn't care?

Disillusioned: Does he seem like he's not just holding you off but is truly turned off by love and marriage as a whole? Him: "I don't know if I believe in love anymore. I'm beginning to think it doesn't really exist—that, like the usefulness of the UN, it's just an illusion."

Demeaning: Is he suddenly belittling you because your boss turned you down for that promotion? Minimizing your contributions to the world?

Understanding Your PF and Your Limits

You also might discover that even if he is marriage minded, his vision of marriage does not exactly harmonize with yours. Jonathan, a thirty-two-year-old implacable taskmaster, opines, "I need to control 80 percent of the marriage. The sex and finances are a must, and the rest we can figure out later. This is nonnegotiable. She can have an opinion, of course, as long as it's not too strong. If she agrees with me, so much the better— then we're both happy. But you always need one dominant person in the marriage, otherwise it will never work. You need that dichotomy." Oh, and he prides himself on never having lost a fight. "No one can win a fight with me." Hmm, sounds like a fun, flexible guy.

If you're dating a PF, who, upon closer inspection, is harboring subconscious thoughts about marriage that you don't like, it's high time to evaluate the stability of your relationship's infrastructure. You must ask yourself:

- Are you prepared to compromise the value you place on your own integrity, morals, and opinions if he imposes his imperiousness on you?
- How long do you think your ulcer of steel can withstand suppressed frustration? Ten, twenty, forty years down the line?
- Do you see yourself growing to like submission?
- Do you genuinely look forward to your marital future?
- Once the balance of power is outlined, would you ever be able to redraw it?

Discovering negative baggage or a misguided sense of superiority may seem like a major disappointment now, but it can serve as your greatest blessing in disguise, as these attitudes are only exacerbated with age. Letting him steamroll over you now is inviting him to steamroll over you the rest of your life—and really not helping the rest of us break any glass ceilings.

As far as relationship tests go, you can dodge only so many bullets and still come out engaged on the other side. So just be yourself—stick to your guns when you feel yourself starting to cave—but at the same time try to embody the wife mold in which you want him to start seeing you. Remember, it's at this "engaged to be engaged" stage that you must capitalize on the subliminal while making a case that he can't refuse. Just make sure you keep your eyes open when you get there. Taking a good hard look at his character—does he take pride in you or take pride in kicking you in the teeth?—will help you determine if this is the right PF in whom to invest so much time and trouble.

16

Shopping for Rings

Relationships are generally moving in a direction; the ones that stay stagnant are the ones that fail to thrive. They're either moving forward or backward—with some sort of identifiable trajectory. Or, to put a guy-friendly spin on it: "A relationship's like a shark; it's gotta keep moving or it's gonna die." If you've been together for more than a year and things are moving forward happily, then squander no time in whipping out that map of better jewelry stores within a three-mile radius of your home. You told that salesperson you'd be back—and now she owes you an apology and ten bucks. Be honest, you've had your eye on at least one store, where you fantasized, "That's where I want my ring to come from when I find the right guy." That said, too many women fall into the

insidious trap of fixating on the ring rather than the relationship itself.

   This chapter will examine these crucial questions: Are
you putting too much focus on your ring and not enough on
your relationship? What says you're engaged: a ring or his
word? And when is the right time to make that first nose-
pressed-against-the-glass visit to Tiffany's? (Hint: be very
careful with this one.)

Shattered Glass: When Premature Window-Shopping Makes Him (or You) Crack

Karen, twenty-eight, is happily married—to the man she met
after her last PF, who seemed like he was on track to being the
one, until he suffered a mini–panic attack during their first
engagement ring window-shopping expedition. It's the all
too common ring-shopping combustion: when proposal
pressure heats up, your PF melts down. "He's what I would
consider a commitment-phobe," she says now. Either that or
the guy's seriously allergic to diamonds. "He was visibly uncomfortable in the store," she recalls, "like he couldn't wait to
get out of there. What should have been a fun afternoon out-
ing was nerve-racking for both of us. Three weeks later, he
told me he wanted to break up."

   Today, Karen's married to the man who, when they
window-shopped for rings, had not a single involuntary
spasm. They'd been dating for fifteen months and "it felt very
natural," she says. That's when you know you have a keeper.

   Denise, twenty-nine, unexpectedly found herself ring
shopping when she and her PF visited a jewelry store to get a
battery for her watch. "All of a sudden, he suggested we check

to see what ring size I am. I was floored!" Since they'd been dating only about five months, Denise hadn't even expected him to pay the eight dollars for the watch battery, so looking at engagement rings together was a delirious surprise. Unfortunately, that bubble of euphoria burst too quickly to allow her to savor the moment.

What happened with her PF over the next few weeks raised back-pedaling to a new art. He got busy with work, stopped calling as frequently, and made excuses to postpone a three-day weekend getaway they had planned. "What I think happened was that he was thirty-three, his family really liked me, and he probably thought he should be married," reasons Denise. "But then, after weeks of him obviously backing off, I was forced to confront him. He said, 'I think we should take more time between dates,'" she recalls with razor-sharp clarity. "And then he said: 'I think we have to cancel our engagement party,' which floored me because I didn't even know we were engaged!" Here, poor Denise had to absorb the knowledge that she had been engaged without knowing about it and, secondly, that it was broken off already. "It was going to be in Boston," he'd told her, having already shared the good news with friends.

"He never even had a conversation with me telling me that we were engaged! He never proposed," she says, still confounded. "And he'd apparently already told his friends about an engagement party that I didn't even know about! I was wondering if we were in the same relationship!" It would have been hurtful enough if the relationship had devolved without the marriage talk, but it was like falling a thousand feet instead of two hundred, now that talk of marriage had entered their orbit. Denise was left with a crushing sense of having come so close yet ruined her chances without even realizing what was going on.

Ideally, you'll be with a mate who wants the same things as you do at the same time you want them. But you need to be mindful of the fact that this is not always the case. You, as we know, are ready to visit Harry Winston on a moment's notice, but rushing to go ring shopping with him too soon can backfire in a big way. Letting him take the relationship reins and look for the ring on his own accord is the ideal—that way, neither of you feels resentment for being rushed or pushed into something.

Treasured Heirloom or Brand-New Bling: Should You Care?

Congratulations—he's ready to propose! But for some SPSs, it's not time to break out the bubbly just yet—your PF could be recycling a double-duty diamond. It's the age-old question: do you feign excitement over his family heirloom of a cloudy Polish diamond circa old, or do you inject the "Let's start a clean slate together with a really expensive sparkling ring" spiel? But let's face the facts: as an exasperated panicker, who are you to demand anything? Don't be the kind of girl who blows a perfectly good PF just because the bling is less than desirable.

Julie, twenty-six, was caught off guard when her boyfriend at the time sprung upon her his deceased grandmother's bauble from the grave. Well, not literally—she hoped. But it does make one wonder: at what stage in the person's life, or maybe more fittingly *afterlife*, does the rock get reclaimed by the cheapest grandson? "It would be an honor!" stammered a visibly disappointed Julie when she learned she was inheriting a hand-me-down diamond. "But you should have seen the look on his face—the excitement when he told me how much it meant to him," she recalls with a flash of guilt. Of course he was elated—who wouldn't be doing backflips after saving roughly twenty thousand dollars? "I know I should have been glad that we were engaged," she says, "but I'd always wanted my own ring and it's hard to let go of that."

"I would have liked to have picked out the stone myself," confesses Allison, thirty-one, recalling her magical proposal moment. She resents her recycled ring—and still can't get beyond it. When she opened the box, no one could accuse Allison of not lighting up—though it was more like an inferno about to blow. "I think he and his brother split their grandmother's huge stone into two uneven dinky ones, one for each fiancée," she sniffs with poorly masked bitterness. "Every time I look at my brother-in-law's fiancée's bony hand, it annoys me that she got the bigger half!"

That said, not every panicked SPS puts so much stock in whether the stone is new or not. When Ginny's PF proposed, she was staring at the diamond whose facets she already knew by heart. But it wasn't from the storefront of her favorite jewelry store. This rock was from a little closer to home—her dead grandmother's home. Friends wasted no time in inquiring about the third act of her grandmother's ring: "Well, did he at least pay your parents for it?" they'd hiss. But this unflappable former panicker steeled herself against the hordes of bitter SPSs of which she herself had been a proud member until a mere few hours ago. "I knew I'd have a life full of whispering from catty friends. But I'm proud to wear my grandma's engagement stone. It means so much to me to be able to carry it on with my future family." At least some people appreciate an elevated measure of meaning!

If Ginny doesn't mind the recycling of her family diamond, neither should any of her friends. She had the flexibility and perspective to enjoy her given ring—whatever its origins. And for that, she takes even more pleasure in wearing her family stone. When it comes to the stone, some SPSs can be as cold as ice. And lose sight of what's more important—having that new-diamond smell or losing the whiff of a life of loneliness.

How Much Should You Really Care About the Ring?

That's something Sharon, twenty-six, really needs to consider. She tried her best to suppress her misgivings about the engagement ring she squeezed out of Russell when he proposed. And that fine acting performance lasted five glorious minutes into their engagement, when she sweetly asked if he would upgrade the 1-carat stone to a bigger one. "But as soon as I saw it, I knew it was your ring," he offered. Clearly Russell had underestimated his future wife's keen eye for the finer things in life.

If your PF proposes and you find yourself looking at the velvet box in his hands with disappointment, you need to ask yourself: has showing off your ring replaced showing off your fiancé? Which "accessory" is more important to you? Ladies, beggars cannot be choosers. And those of us clocking more than our fair share of miles on panicked terrain know that a ring is a ring is a ring. Whether it's unearthed from the plastic wrapping buried deep inside a cereal box or pried off a deceased relative, who are you to squabble? Let's not get greedy now when our eyes should really be fixed only on the prize: the ring . . . *any* ring.

When I hear an SPS fire off, "If you can't bother to get

me a Tiffany diamond, don't bother proposing!" I wince. She
has the nerve to call herself an SPS and complain about being
unmarried? What chutzpah! If you are genuinely committed
to your PF—and to walking down the aisle—then the color
of the diamond (and the color of its box, for that matter)
shouldn't factor into your decision. Besides, Julie, Allison, and
Ginny have a whole lifetime to point out how their husbands
saved the money and curse the way they want to use the newfound dough. There's a lesson we can all extract from these
heartwarming tales: if you can learn to love your flawed fiancé, you can learn to love his secondhand ring as well.

The Three-Ring Circus

Not all relationships safely weather the ring storm. There are
consequences when your extreme shallowness trumps the
sanctity of your relationship. When Brenda, twenty-five, demanded that her fiancé, Charlie, exchange her first engagement ring, he felt crushed that Brenda didn't love the ring he
had chosen to be an expression of their love. But in the interest of making her happy, he went back anyway. When Brenda
demanded that he then exchange the *second* one because it
had those side stones she always thought overpowered the
main one, he dejectedly slunk back toward the jewelry store.
When Brenda found fault in the third try, the entire affair was
shut down for good. Turns out, Brenda wasn't the ringmaster
of this circus as she thought—Charlie was, and he called off
the engagement. Brenda's third chance at redemption turned
out to be her last. And despite desperate pleas for Charlie to
take her back, he told Brenda that in the weeks he'd assidu-
ously tried to please her with her fantasy ring, he discovered
a side of her that he didn't want to marry.

"I remember we checked out a caterer for the wedding reception and the director asked when we got engaged," Charlie recalls. "And before I could answer, Brenda told her that we weren't really engaged yet because she didn't have 'quite the right ring.' " They'd dated for three years, but it was in the month he searched desperately for the perfect ring that he realized what was really important to Brenda. And he shuddered at what he saw. "The fact that I went out there three times to try to make her happy wasn't enough for her," Charlie said. "After a while, I realized it wasn't about 'us' anymore, it was all about the ring. That's when it was over for me."

You don't want to suffer a relationship casualty because of the ring. Getting so caught up in the "right ring" eclipses what's truly important: an actual guy who's willing to marry you. If you have the right guy, any ring he proposes with should be the right one.

Ring shopping should never be rushed—on either person's end. And as eager as we are to examine diamonds with that cool little single binocular that jewelers use, remember that it all comes down to timing—on your gun-shy PF's behalf as well as your own. And when, or if, the time is right, don't fret too much about the ring he produces. Remember, in the end it's not really about the ring per se; it's about what the ring says: "My fiancé loves me more than anything in the world—and he's made a killing in the East Asian markets!"

17

"We're Engaged! It's Just Something You Say . . ."

George Costanza immortalized this timeless nugget on *Seinfeld* when he tried to weasel out of his engagement to his girlfriend Susan in order to date the much-feted Marisa Tomei, but it does have a relevant place in today's dating world. After all the hunting and manipulating, it's easy to feel like it's all been building up to this. You got the guy, the proposal, and the ring. Time to take your victory lap, right?

Not so fast. Sometimes the panic spurs us on so fast that we don't really stop to look around until we reach the final destination. And when we get there we find that our initial euphoria is dampened by the nagging truth—this isn't the right relationship.

This chapter will examine how to know when an engagement is really an engagement; how to figure out if he's *re-*

ally the right one; what you should do when you have second thoughts; and how discovering that "engaged" isn't the be-all and end-all can help you learn how to live simultaneously single *and* panic free.

Are You Really Engaged?

Sometimes, surprisingly, the answer is blurrier than you'd think. I mean, how can we not recognize the most anticipated four-word aria of our life, "Will you marry me?" when we hear it? But semantics can play a more pivotal role in your engagement than you'd expect. When my old PF broached the subject of marriage, he oftentimes blurred the line between intellectualizing it and actualizing it, creating such bleeding between "theory" and "practice" that it was hard for me to distinguish if he'd actually popped the question or not. "How do you want to be proposed to?" he'd ask. Or, "Where would you want to get married?" Was that a proposal? Am I engaged? Am I at least semi-engaged? Am I supposed to read between the blurry lines here? My index finger was poised over the caterer's number on speed dial—I only wished he'd tell me what he wanted!

The next day's dawn, though, inevitably cleared up most of the confusion, as he seemed to always be infected with amnesia of the heart, with no mention of our new engagement, and apparently no announcement in the paper. He became the boy who cried engagement!

A friend of mine once casually mentioned that her sister was getting engaged next month. "Oooh, that's . . . great," I stammered. Yet it struck me as odd: if the girl already knows when she's getting engaged—if they've already talked about it in that kind of detail—then isn't that an engagement? "They're getting the ring in a few weeks," she explained.

An engagement is an agreement—sometimes brought about under duress with the use of anesthetics—but it's an agreement nonetheless. It's not—as we've learned—strictly about the ring. It's not about the ring, and it's not about the empty rhetoric, either; it's about mutually agreeing to wed— and making it actionable.

How Sure Are *You*? Forget How Right It Looks, How Right Does It Feel?

When couples feel they have something to prove, they often tout to an unreasonable degree the amount of time they spend together: "Jeff and I are inseparable! He won't even let me go to the bathroom with the door closed." Well, maybe that speaks more to Jeff's suspicion you are using drugs than to the strength of your togetherness. Ditto for those overly amorous couples who seek others' admiration and jealousy. Ultimately, when you're in a solid relationship, you shouldn't feel like you have something to prove to the greater population about your happiness with your PF. And if there is an element of showboating "your love," then it probably underscores a need to prove something to yourself even more than the need to prove it to the world.

Okay, but It Feels Close to Right. Can't I Just Let It Slide?

Sometimes, in our rush to seal the deal and be settled already, we force ourselves to overlook the nagging doubts that linger in the far reaches of our minds. This is the panicker's biggest challenge—to keep your panic and desire for the fairy-tale ending in check long enough to evaluate each relationship for what it really is. So is it panic or true love that's driving the bus? Here is a checklist to use before you make one of the biggest decisions of your life:

- Do you feel comfortable with him—completely at ease, never anxious or agitated?
- Do you trust him wholly—with your emotions, finances, feelings, unlocked diary, cookie dough in the fridge that you asked him not to eat except in case of emergency?
- Do you say to yourself, "Sometimes it's even better when we don't talk," and truly mean it as a compliment? Those quiet shared moments when you're not talking to each other can be just as powerful, if not more so, than when you do.
- Do you feel confident that even if someday he discovers you aren't perfect, you'll still be enough for him just by being yourself?

If you feel good after a genuine analysis of your relationship, you're most likely with the right PF. But if you're living a lie in a factitious relationship, even though everyone else seems to be buying its authenticity, it's time to wake up to reality: you can't ignore these gaping relationship holes forever—and you need to figure out if this is the person with whom you're supposed to be.

Sometimes, a relationship suffers chronic symptoms that go undetected even by you. If you're unsure, ask your female friends—preferably happily married ones, not competitive SPSs—if they think this guy's the one—and really listen to what they say.

My friend Nadine, who is an inch away from taking the marital plunge, has found the résumé of her dreams. Now, if only she had the fiancé to match it. She thinks she's happy, but I have a sneaking suspicion her fiancé is failing to satisfy her. She'd always been one of those girls for whom the term "formidable sex fiend" is an understatement. In fact, Nadine could probably run sexual circles around most oat-sowing guys her age. I thought it was disturbing enough when this sexaholic confessed she'd downshifted to having sex only once a week with her fiancé, until the newest red flag waved ominously: she hasn't gotten a bikini wax in six months! This was a blatant cry for help!

Yet, I know she still wants to get married—even to him. But the sex diet this former booty binger has been on does raise some alarming questions. If she's willingly starving herself of sex, what other vital relationship nutrients is she sacrificing as well? The only aphrodisiac that excited her was him being open about wanting to marry her—from their first date, in fact. He was never shy about the fact that she was the woman for him. When he threw a party at his apartment right after they first started dating, a mutual friend of ours enviously whispered to Nadine, "Wow, when is all of this going to be yours?"

Well, Nadine never asked for my opinion and went ahead and accepted when her now-fiancé proposed. She may never derive a mind-blowing orgasm again, but at least we know she'll be in the throes of financial ecstasy for the rest of her life.

It's far from the matrimonial kiss of death for women to evaluate—perhaps many times, from many angles—their grounds for getting married. In fact, it demonstrates a real sense of maturity and self-awareness to address the authenticity of your so-called solid relationship. To go through your life avoiding the essential questions is to turn a blind eye to possible emotional anemia. Having the guts to confront areas most women would love to sidestep forever and forcing yourself to examine your fiancé and your future life together is something every woman owes herself before taking the plunge.

It's what overcoming the Panic Years and being in the control room of your life is all about! If you are too scared to open that Pandora's box, for fear of unearthing deeply buried problems, I guarantee you will wish that you had tackled every square inch of your relationship now before those problems unfailingly surface down the line.

If we are to be fully truthful with ourselves, no bride-to-be ever says with 100 percent assurance that she's made the right choice; no one has the prescience of 100 percent accuracy. Marriage is always a leap of faith, and part of the excitement is the very sense of the unknown future that is wide open to you. Yet, your future shouldn't feel like a coin toss either—a fifty-fifty chance of happiness. When someone tells me, "I don't have to think about it, we're perfect together," I see red flags. Not necessarily for their relationship, which may or may not survive, but for someone too arrogant to see if she and the relationship can withstand some deeper scrutiny.

Finding the Strength to Walk Away

Just like the confounding pairing of TomKat, the onetime panicker who breaks off an engagement provides us with one of those unanswerable questions capable of confounding every philosopher, scientist, and think tank in America: *why would you do it?*

I arranged for a private interview, and after their keepers unlocked their glass displays, I talked to the runaway fiancées we'd hear about only in an occasional horror flick, but never really thought existed. Even more shocking than realizing that their flesh looks like yours and mine (only, of course, less elastic) is the alarming but undeniable awareness that they can actually pass for satisfied, content, well-adjusted people. Dare I suggest even more so than your garden variety SPS?

Not one formerly engaged person whom I spoke to failed to express her relief that she walked away, knowing it wasn't right, regardless of whether or not she was currently coupled or single. Knowing in the inner reaches of your heart that your fiancé is not the right one and making a move to end it takes both Herculean courage and a really reliable getaway car.

Mandi, thirty-two, smiles with almost unabashed glee when she recalls walking away from her fiancé. "I was twenty-nine and a half when I met my him. After the first date, I practically skipped into work the next morning, singing to my coworker that I just met the man I was going to marry. I thought to myself, 'Finally! I finally found him.' I guess in hindsight I wanted to get married so badly that I got ahead of myself and forced it."

Fast-forward six months: "It was my thirtieth birthday— and I was experiencing the usual reflective thoughts that come with that milestone—and he took me to this incredibly elegant restaurant. We had a beautiful dinner and he took me back to his apartment to give me his gift. He's a musician, so it was fitting that it was a framed gift of his liner notes from a song he composed for me. And I just thought he was doing this because it was my birthday. But then . . . out of nowhere, he proposed. In my head, I was like, 'Um, Oh, okay . . . , um, sure!' " Mandi was far from certain, but taken completely by surprise she accepted, even though neither of them had really discussed the idea of marriage before.

Then came the hollow gestures of gratitude, as Mandi prayed her tear ducts wouldn't fail her. "At that point, I made myself cry," she recalls, "because I thought crying was what you were supposed to do when you get engaged."

The engagement lasted four months, during which there were enough real tears to last a lifetime of marriage. "I was so upset during that time that I started seeing a therapist and she helped me realize that I needed to call it off." All the while, through all her doubts and depression, Mandi's mom was happy as a clam planning the engagement party and wedding full steam ahead, completely oblivious, or worse, completely insensitive to her daughter's grave doubts.

The process of planning a wedding is often said to be a predictor of your life together, and Mandi's situation was no exception. In the months that followed the proposal, her learning curve was compressed, as she was forced to digest volumes about her fiancé and his family, for better or worse, without any time to chew or swallow. "One day," she recalls, "we fought for about eight hours over the appropriateness of a cheese wheel at the cocktail hour. I just got a flash forward of the rest of my life and I didn't like what I saw. I saw the next fifty years of my life with this man and I didn't like it. I realized that if we were fighting to the death over cheese wheels, I could only imagine how the slightly more impor-tant decisions like family and kids would go."

But it was her own behavior as much as her fiancé's that tipped her off. "At one point I said, 'You should have saved for a bigger ring,' which is so not a me thing to say," admits Mandi. It was an epiphany, a clear-cut sign that something was grossly wrong with the relationship because intellectually she knew that a ring shouldn't matter. That it did matter to her signified greater problems. Mandi knew when to call it a day and show the Panic who was boss. "I was so focused on the wedding day that I wasn't thinking enough about the rest of my life. And that's an extremely dangerous mistake that too many girls make. Now, with my new boyfriend, I couldn't care less about a wedding. What I care about is the two of us."

Life Post-Engagement: Single, but Panic-Free

Feeling revitalized in heart and mind, Mandi was sure that she'd made the right decision. "After I broke it off, I felt so free! I literally felt like a new person. I didn't date for months and I didn't even care. I was just happy sitting on the couch, watching TV. I finally came into my own. Now I don't want to get married just because. My friends are all married and they aren't any happier because of it. If I met my current boyfriend five or even three years ago, I probably would have passed him over. I probably would have said something completely sur- face and lame, like 'Well, he's not established enough,' and it's taken me all that's happened to realize that's not important. It's not just about having a guy who's able to provide for me. I'm a working girl who does well for herself and I can take care of myself.

"Years ago I would have been so caught up with 'is he a doctor or lawyer?' I just loved that idea of a professional, of this older, more 'sophisticated' guy who would wear a suit to work every day." Now it makes Mandi laugh to think that she actually used to care more about a power suit and a beefy portfolio than her connection with the actual person.

"I'd reject guys for the stupidest reasons: he liked New Jersey, he wore tapered jeans, he owned a cat named Cleo." (Well, still valid reasons perhaps, but nevertheless . . .) After a while, she didn't even know what her type was anymore. "I realize now that the reason I so flatly rejected these nice guys was because on some level I knew I wasn't ready. This, despite my head (and my mom, and my friends) telling me it was time to settle down. When it's right, you just know. But with my ex-fiancé, the only thing keeping us together was the excitement of the wedding; it wasn't about the two of us.

"Nowadays, I occasionally pass by the jewelry store where my engagement ring is in the window," she admits. And she hasn't winced once.

What We Can Learn

As wrenching as it is to break off an engagement, it could be the best decision you'll ever make. To acknowledge the mismatch before the wedding is always better than realizing it after . . . and having to get yet another set of monogrammed towels. And sometimes just saying you were once engaged adds to your mystique exponentially. After all, it's much cooler than saying you're divorced.

Sometimes, when we're in the throes of the Panic, when we're so focused on achieving what we think we want, we neglect what we really need—time for ourselves, to nurture ourselves and discover who we are and who we want to be, regardless of our marital status. How can you possibly achieve that when you devote all your time and mental and emotional energy to finding a PF? You'll be hunting for a PF to suit the personality you don't even know you have!

Finding a PF who's willing to marry you at the height of your Panic Years frenzy carries the risk of seriously clouded judgment. If you actually do find that PF before you find yourself, and years later find yourselves diverging in so many ways because you (and he) aren't the people you thought you were years ago, don't say I didn't warn you!

We sometimes expect to have a crystallized moment when we're magically going to know if a particular person is the one, but really it's more complicated—more nuanced—than that. Anyone knows that the potent feeling of today might not be the potent feeling of tomorrow, so it should take much more than a fleeting magical feeling to make something like committing to marriage a reality. It's widely acknowledged that women possess greater self-awareness and intuition than men, so maximize the natural gifts with which you were hard-wired and navigate your way through external murkiness to discover your internal core of clarity.

It's the fundamental lesson every SPS needs to understand: hastily committing to a man and a marriage isn't overcoming the Panic Years; in fact, it's just the opposite—it's surrendering to them. The Panic Years do exist—and you can recognize that without tearing your hair out. But you can also rise above them and conquer them—ring or no ring. At least *you* get to make that call! Mandi genuinely surmounted the Panic Years—it may have taken her a broken engagement and the chilling notion of a cheese wheel to confront her buried issues, but she did it. For Mandi, living a life without a ring right now is fine—she's doing what's best for her at this stage in her life and it feels great.

Part
III

The Silver Lining in

Being Single

Life *before* marriage: does such a concept actually exist? Part III reinforces the importance of savoring the precious time "alone" until you do get married, as it is time you'll never get back once you're hitched. It reminds you to enjoy your youth and your friends and this opportunity to focus on becoming the best version of yourself. Women who are so overcome by their own panic damage more than just the down pillows they punch every night in frustration—they damage their emotional psyche. They end up wasting years, and panic becomes a great detriment to their ultimate dating and life goals.

This section serves as a reminder that you shouldn't feed into the Panic just because your friends are happy and attached, and conversely that you shouldn't feel joy because your friends are just as panicked as you are. It's about reminding yourself to go at your own pace and not compare yourself to people in your social circle who might have a different time frame.

While your PF probably won't magically appear, if you continue doing the things you enjoy doing, you may just find the counterpart you didn't realize you were looking for in the first place. It will be more fluid and a lot less forced. You've always wanted to try welding class to explore your artistic bent; there just might be a PF in your class who's lured in by the soothing sounds of a rumbling sandblaster—a match made in Apex Technical School heaven! As we saw in the last section, what we must strive to avoid is letting the Panic seep into our skin so deeply that we marry someone for the sake of getting married and then down the line end up resenting him to the point where we refer to him as "Sperm Donor" instead of "Daddy" in front of the kids.

18

The Grass Isn't
Always Greener

The grass is always greener—in any situation. And life is no different when it comes to marriage. The perfect life you think your friend has because she's settled down rarely matches the reality.

When your married girlfriend tells you that going to the market to return sour cottage cheese on a Saturday night and training the dog to refrain from peeing on the new Pottery Barn sofa are her most exciting activities, your envy inevitably starts to dissipate. There's a reason that SAPs (the Settled and Pious) don't want to talk about their lives—the faulty sump pump and other fun domestic trappings. They're the ones living vicariously through you! Instead, they want to hear about your exciting dating debacles. Savor these moments of having people hang on your every word while they still find you nouveau charming—because once you're married, no one's going to want to suffer through your rants about your own cottage cheese fiascos and your laments over your husband's LDL/HDL levels.

This chapter will reveal the truth about your friends' underwhelming married lives and share stories of real-life SPSs who wouldn't have their singledom any other way.

She May Not Be Single Anymore, but She's Not Set for Life Either

Adrienne, thirty-one, would love to be transported back in time, not just to have purchased that killer BCBG leather coat in 2004 that still keeps her up at night, but to have reminded herself to enjoy her twenties instead of getting entangled in a sticky web of marriage-mindedness. "Once you're married, you're married," she leans in and whispers sotto voce, like she's divulging the location of Jimmy Hoffa's resting place. Seems obvious, sure, but what's implied is that once your single days are sealed, gone are the days of "me," "me time," and "me not having homicidal thoughts if he leaves the refrigerator door open one more time." Everything is in terms of "we" now. "*We* have a joint checking account. *We* loved/hated the movie. *We* shouldn't leave sharp objects around our five-hundred-square-foot claustrophobic living space whose walls are slowly closing in on us because *we* don't trust ourselves not to slice each other."

Gloria Steinem—to whom I'm eternally grateful for helping to make lax shaving fashionable again—said it best when she shone the spotlight on women's self-imposed pressure to get married. While no one has a crystal ball, she said, if women were assured that by thirty-five they'd have the husband of their dreams, they could breathe easier and actually let themselves enjoy their lives. Simply having faith that it will "work out" is sometimes just the blanket of reassurance we all need to wrap ourselves in—and actually allow us to enjoy dating!

Marriage: Heaven or Just Anticlimactic as Hell?

Sari waited two agonizingly long years (which is really nine in Panic Years) to squeeze a proposal out of her PF. Few people were more determined than Sari, or more dedicated. No matter the topic, she artfully managed to steer any meandering conversation safely back to her comfort zone: marriage talk. Expressing disgust over the pesky Middle East crisis? Sari handily brought it back to the core issue: "not enough happy Middle Eastern marriages." So, when she finally did land her diamond and her dream, no one was more surprised than she was to discover how anticlimactic the moment was. After her aggressive emotional and mental investment over the past two years, the payoff could not have been any more underwhelming. Underneath that shimmering patina of celebration lay a sizable dose of disappointment.

Opening up, she admitted that once married, all the buildup and anticipation she'd created left her with an empty feeling she couldn't shake. "I was afraid life after the wedding would be boring, marriage would be boring and that I would become boring—and I think my worst fears are coming true." Well, as Sari's friend, I can't say she has become *that* excruciating to be around, except when she's lamenting about the following: "Yesterday, Marc and I picked out twin burial plots together. It's less fun than it sounds. On a Saturday morning in my single days, I would be having brunch with my girlfriends while flirting with guys over mimosas!" Something about her tone made me think she actually wanted to be *in* that burial plot right now.

So maybe this new nuptialed life isn't always better than our current life after all. "Couples therapy is going really well," my newlywed friend of ten months offered when I inquired, perking up noticeably. "I think we're really working out our issues and learning to be more respectful of each other." Hmm, couples therapy really does sound like twice the fun. And then there's my one SAP friend whose one-year-old marriage is really killing her social life: "I need a night out dancing at a club again in a slutty outfit," she wails. "I'm going crazy!!"

Friendship Absenteeism: It Goes Both Ways

Marriage seems to have the same effect on almost all women who enter into it. They may make fine wives, but they become lousy friends. When your SAP friends come crawling back after months of friendship absenteeism, it's hard not to feel resentful. "Do you want to do dinner this weekend? Scott's out of town on business so I have some time," one lamely asked me a few weeks ago. "Don't do me any favors!" I hissed to myself.

Yes, the transparency of her rare invitations makes your blood boil. And yes, you instinctively want to give her an excuse and tell her you have some fabulous, can't-miss movie premiere your friend in PR has invited you to. (Everyone gets jealous over movie premieres, especially when you inject "Keanu" to the point of excess.) But if you're the slightest bit inclined to salvage the friendship—and you really should be!—then you should cut your friend some slack. She may have a good twenty pounds on you since she got married and let herself go, but you can still be the bigger person here. Besides, most women will tell you that post-wedding, maintaining the balance between their husband and their friends is hard. You may feel like she's abandoned the flock, but more than likely she feels a certain sadness at being sidelined from you and the life she used to have.

When a friend gets married, it's naturally going to be an adjustment for everyone, but there's no need to cut her off when she's struggling to balance all areas of her life. While you might be someone who bruises easily and the one time your married friend flakes on dinner plans makes you feel like swearing off your friendship, try to recognize that she still needs you in her life. You can't punish her just because she's married and use any small slipup on her part to cut the cord. Remember that you both need each other—and her husband can never replace a good friend.

Single and Not Just Surviving, but Thriving!

Judy, a family friend who "was in her forties once," is a permanent bachelorette and she's keen on keeping it that way. While her coupled friends in all their marital haughtiness privately deride her as someone who's "alone and pathetic," my own family included (I'm regularly warned, "You don't want to wind up a Judy"), I look at this woman and see someone who has found true happiness all on her own.

Mention this to my mom and she instinctively snaps, "Oh, that's a cover, can't you see that? Who's in a French club for fun?!" Still, the bon vivant's date book is always filled, she is actually friends with someone who had a castle named after him in Budapest, and when she's invited for special occasions by friends and family, it's never out of pity but because people genuinely enjoy her company. She also lives in an amazing rent-controlled Tribeca apartment that she can decorate however she pleases.

And it's not hard to see through her married friends' thin veneer of superiority. Jealousy, even resentment, over Judy's freedom—with her great apartment and exotic world travel—forces them to overcompensate by deriding her so outwardly. It's my own mom who has longed to live a fast-paced life in the city—the same thing that Judy's been doing for the last twenty years. When she incessantly snickers about the amount of work Judy's apartment needs—in addition to maligning her lifestyle—she inadvertently tips her hand, revealing how envious she actually is of her "poor friend."

"If I feel alone, it's not because I don't have a husband," Judy has always said. "Plenty of my married friends feel more isolated than most single women like me who've learned self-reliance from being on their own for so long. You're pitied, unless of course you're a celebrity—single celebrities are available celebrities and their public profile soars!" Now that I think about it, I haven't heard anyone call Diane Keaton a spinster in a while.

Voices from the Other Side

Is it enlightenment or apocalypse? You decide. No, they're not dead, not phantoms or ghosts. But to many, they verge on the realm of extraterrestrial. They're the "single and happy" set— the other camp—speaking out here. Now, the grandes dames of secure singles break their silence. So you're single at twenty-nine—is it a fate worse than crow's-feet or still better than a ring from Sam's Club? For these aging liberators, it's neither! Below, wisdom from the faction in no particular rush to bury their single persona.

Gillian, thirty-two: "I thank God I didn't get married at twenty-two, a week after I graduated college, like my sister did. She's divorced now, and in hindsight it seems almost inevitable. I changed so much in my twenties and I'm definitely not the same person I was then. It would have been a huge mistake to get locked into something that young and then have your path diverge from your husband's years later."

Reina, twenty-eight: "As a kid, I always looked at marriage as bliss, but looking at some of my married friends now, I wouldn't want any of their lives. They think marriage is an accomplishment, a personal achievement. If you asked any of them, they'd say their lives are fulfilled. But I think I'm doing more with my life."

Linda, twenty-eight: "I'm in no rush to get married. I'm not an old maid; in fact, I have a maid. I have it made! I'm very happy with my life and my career."

Renay, twenty-nine: "Ninety-five percent of my friends are married. It started happening when I was twenty-five—that was the turning point and it has only gained momentum from there. It was the number one priority for most of them, but, if anything, it's driven me away from getting married. I've seen what they've traded off—freedom, flexibility, a passion for their career, an opportunity to really know themselves and discover who they are. Yes, at some point I definitely want to be married, just not at the expense of anything else. You always have to make sacrifices in a relationship, but I would be willing to give things up only if I knew without a doubt that the man was worth it."

Shira, thirty-one: "Women are just so much more beautiful, inside and out, once they turn thirty. They're calmer, they're more confident, they're not running out every night giving themselves whiplash to see 'Is he the one for me? Is he?' I'm so glad I'm not married because the guys I knew back then are not the kind of people I can see myself spending the rest of my life with now. My long-term plan even a few years ago was so different from my long-term plan now—thank God I didn't get locked into anything before I knew what I really wanted."

Becca, twenty-seven: "I've been sooo inundated with marriage lately. A lot of my friends (mostly late twenties) are getting married soon. In the meantime, many of my friends aged thirty to forty are in the midst of getting divorced. And my younger friends (early to mid-twenties) are bitching about how they want to get married. It's just driving me crazy, primarily because it's just not something you should build your life around. When it happens, it happens. Why rush and get all bent out of shape in the meantime?"

Elana, twenty-seven: "I have a nickname among my friends. So whenever I see it's one of them calling, I always answer the phone, 'Hello, single and loving it . . . .' That's the nickname they've given me!"

Candice, twenty-eight: "I always knew that I didn't want to get married young; I wanted to be out on my own and be independent before I attached myself to anyone. Women are oh-so-excited about putting a rock on their finger, yet they seem to forget where the tradition came from. That diamond is a sign of ownership. It's part of the contract. 'You agree to marry me, and I give you this rock to symbolize I own you.' It's a down payment. In an age of women's lib and whatnot, why do so many vapid women want this symbol? As for me, I'd rather get a red velvet engagement sofa."

Jenifour, twenty-seven: "I hope to God that I'm thirty and not married—if I'm so lucky! I have nothing against marriage—I want to get married someday—but I'm too young now. There's just too much of my life to live. Every new day that I'm not married and don't have kids is a day I'm grateful for. I'm so happy to be single now and living my life; I love being responsible for only myself. I think the only way I'm going to get married is if the guy can't take it anymore and really needs to marry me—and I love him so much that I cave."

Marcy, twenty-seven: She thought she was doing MLK proud by "living the dream." Okay, so his dream could have been construed as slightly loftier than hers, but hers was a dream nonetheless—one that was close to being realized. She and her PF were window-shopping for engagement rings when all of a sudden she pulled what we think may be the first documented U.S. case of a woman pulling a reverse-panicked moment, a female prematrimonial meltdown. "My longtime boyfriend was pushing marriage on me. I'm actually pretty averse to the idea of marriage and children—to me it's always seemed like a cage. And I thought our love could transcend that and I could get over it, but in the end I guess I couldn't. I was forced to break up with him, as painful as it was."

The Secure Spinster: How Is This Rare Specimen Hardwired and What Is She Smoking?

We're going deeper inside the mind of the single girl who doesn't want marriage. "I was always honest with my ex-boyfriend about my lack of desire to have biological children and my neutral feelings toward marriage," says Erin, twenty-eight. "However, I think he felt that he could change my mind on both fronts and to a certain extent, he succeeded, though not to the extent that he would have wished. We dated for three years and during the last year, I began to get very swayed by those around me cooing over the prospect of a proposal (though I was always clear that I would never wear an engagement ring unless my fiancé did as well, which he agreed to). But once we moved in together, I saw what marriage would mean. Though we had an egalitarian relationship, he expected me to do the household chores that required daily maintenance, while he did the gendered work that was needed on a weekly basis, like taking the garbage out and making repairs. At this point, all of my previous concerns about marriage came back full force. So we broke up. I understand that my feelings toward marriage might change at some point, but as of right now, the idea repulses me."

Yes, it's the needle in a haystack, the reluctant bride. But if the single girl can't make room for marriage in her heart or her life, then there should be no societal double standard imposed on her; just as we give latitude to marriage-phobic men, we too should extend the same latitude to their female counterparts. And good for those girls for staying true to themselves—and may the rest of the Marcys and Erins out there find the right blend of love they're looking for.

Rising Above It All

One day I was occupying a cozy little corner in Barnes & Noble perusing the latest issue of *In Style Weddings* (just because you're not officially picking out crystal bowls or flatware doesn't mean you can't indulge in a harmless fantasy or two) when a long-lost (but not enough) married friend bounced over to me, gushing: "Doree, oh that's so wonderful you're getting married!"

"Um, well not yet, it's preparation," I stammered.

"Oh, wow, who's the guy you're dating?" she asks, her unkind eyes surveying me head to toe.

"Well, he's kind of inflatable, but very well-mannered and I get along great with his air pump," I quipped. As she walked away, I could hear her bereaved whisper, "Oh, that's so sad."

And you know what? I didn't care—not about the stigma of "getting caught" reading the magazine and I didn't care that the nuptially haughty bitch pitied me. I just laughed—and in that moment, I realized I didn't care what she, or anyone else, thought about me or my marital status. It's all too easy for other people to eyeball you for five seconds and pass judgment on your life so they don't have to think about their own. Don't pay any mind to it. Confidence isn't chiding a single person because she's reading a wedding magazine; it's the single person reading the wedding magazine who has the true confidence—to actually think about what she wants for her future. I felt perfectly content with myself that day; in fact, it was my old friend who I kind of started to pity, because, when you think about it, she may not really have any more dreams to dream now that her life is tied up in a bow at twenty-seven. For once, I didn't feel envious.

There is much to look forward to in your life right now—ring or no ring. And you shouldn't need to hear laments from SAPs who secretly miss their "old lives" to perk you up—although it certainly doesn't hurt. Knowing that you have the very life that most of these women wish they could relive is a pretty good feeling and a reminder to enjoy these days. So relish the world of possibility that is before you—and the fact that unlike your married friends, you don't have to rely on "appointment sex."

19

"To Thine Own Self Be True" and Other Shakespearean Crap

When you so single-mindedly try to achieve something—i.e., marriage—with complete tunnel vision it's all too easy to lose sight of why you wanted it so urgently in the first place. Therefore, it is essential to create goals for yourself beyond that of marriage at this point in your life. Marriage can certainly be a means to an end; it can, after all, afford riches like love and children and an enviable home whose enormity requires aerial shots to fully capture. But, it cannot be The End—the only goal you've set for yourself with nothing left to accomplish in life, no achievement left to tackle. While being connected to a lifelong partner can be a transcendent experience, it is not The End, and recognizing the difference is essential. Because after all the gifts are opened and the annoying champagne flutes displayed and you start to feel a wallop of that "what now?" feeling creeping up in your throat, if you have not created goals beyond this point, you're going to hit the wall—and shatter all your new china in the process.

This chapter explores the delusions about matrimony that plague many an SPS, and why staying true to yourself is ultimately your fastest ticket out of the Panic Years once and for all.

Whole vs. Hole—Can You Tell the Difference?

The old Shakespearean phrase "panicking is such sweet sorrow" has never rung truer than it does today. Sometimes, failure to achieve what isn't meant to be is precisely what brings you closer to your intended path. So, consider this not time wasted, but an invaluable opportunity for learning about yourself, finding your core strengths, and putting them to good use!

There are many valid forms of unhealthy escapism that I cheerfully espouse—jaunts to Las Vegas's high-stakes tables, *Golden Girls* marathons on Lifetime, polishing your tinfoil action figure collection—but people all too often lean on marriage as one of them. Marriage should not be the natural outgrowth of avoidance. Take a more global look at your life and at yourself; busying yourself by getting married is the ultimate short-term way to fill the real holes in your life.

Take a good introspective look at the essence of marriage and the reasons you want to marry at all. If it's a quest for an identity, a way to define yourself—as a wife, or a luxury SUV–loving suburban lady of leisure who lunches at the country club—then that may be something you want to examine further with your personal team of specialists before pledging yourself to the first guy who asks.

SPS delusion: "I hate being single because I don't have anyone who I try to be my best for, and I truly miss that."
Reality check: The only person you need to be your best self for is you. Because, ultimately, trying to please someone else never works. So cut out the middleman and target the real beneficiary—*you!*

Seven reasons *not* to get married:

- You need to find an identity and you need to find one fast.
- It's about time you enjoy the cushy, halcyon life you haven't earned.
- You're already alone now, why not be alone with some annoying guy you're not compatible with who shares the expenses and gets you on his health insurance?
- Food will taste better, the air will feel purer, colors will no longer be muted.
- You've got nothing better to do, you really don't. Why not make the biggest commitment you can ever make, and even drag some unsuspecting guy into the equation, just because it sounds like something you should do?
- Your lease is about to expire, along with your patience. Is this a sign from above that the timing is just right?

- The most unattractive girl at work just got engaged, driving home the new dictum "You don't have to be mildly offensive looking to get married, but it does help."

Anyone Can Get Married—The Question Is, Do You Really Want To?

When I say anyone, I mean anyone. We've all seen those un-reasonably annoying kids trolling about. You think they're lab created? They must be spawned somewhere . . . The sad truth is that getting married doesn't require:

- Strong character
- Genuine concern for others
- Emotional intelligence
- Mental intelligence
- Good genetic makeup
- Good makeup application
- Thoughtfulness

In fact, getting married is easy; it's keeping it together over a lifetime that's the hard part. So it's not a question of how badly you want it, it's *why* you do.

One of my male friends, Len, twenty-six, is confident that any woman—if she really wants to—can get married. "The girlfriend I was dating eight months before she got engaged to someone else probably has no deeper connection with her fiancé than she had with me," he says. Len attributes her re-cent engagement to timing: "She's not a particularly thought-ful person and in all the time we dated the relationship never really got below the surface. I don't think her relationship with her fiancé is any more special or meaningful than ours was. I just think he happened to want to get married when she did." But is this what you really want?

We all coo when we see those wrinkled, crinkled oldster couples inching their way down the street and melt, saying "Oooh, I really want that!" But first, it's essential to understand how they got there, why they're pulling each other out of harm's way instead of thrusting each other into oncoming traffic, and how hard they had to work at maintaining their connection. Most have likely survived more hardships than happiness, endured more pitfalls than parties, but to see their love—and not only their weight—balloon together over the years is really what it's all about: companionship that thrives when you're no longer firm and tight and when reconstructive surgeons would reject you as a patient. This kind of relationship takes a depth of feeling, understanding, and connection that can't be willed into being by sheer desire, or by standing in front of an altar taking vows. So don't put the cart before the horse—marriage isn't the ticket to love and happiness; happiness with yourself and with your life is the ticket to finding love that lasts a lifetime.

Stop Annoying Your Friends

If letting go of the Panic for philosophical reasons is still too much of a struggle for you, then heed this very practical piece of advice: No one will want to be your friend if you continue to be annoying. There are enough environmental pollutants in the atmosphere to contend with: carbon dioxide emissions and the new Justin Timberlake cologne aren't helping matters. But your sour frame of mind is equally at fault for contaminating the otherwise sweet mood of those around you. You are now officially noise pollution personified. Leaking your egregiously negative energy into the airstream will leave friends—married or not—no choice but to habitually screen your calls like you're a relentless telemarketer. Do you want your sneering friends whispering behind your back? The phrase "I'm hoping she gets married soon so she'll just shut up!" has crossed my disloyal lips on more than one occasion.

Every time a panicked friend asks, "Do you think I'll be alone forever? Even if I get married at thirty-two, that's not good enough! I need to be married by twenty-eight!" I throw her a life jacket and assure her that an amazing woman like her won't sit on the shelf long (I don't have the heart to point out that she hasn't been twenty-eight in two years). But patience and consolation wear thin on even the most compassionate confidantes.

So rein yourself in now before the panic becomes polarizing. If you think panicking en masse with the P. Posse is demoralizing, imagine having alienated even fellow SPSs who can't bear your particular brand of self-pity; this admonition from atop my panic pulpit comes not as a self-righteous sermon, but from personal experience. (I had to drop an SPS who self-pitied herself out of the party.) You don't want to be someone who the world sees only through the prism of Panic.

To Thine Own Self Be True

I was doing very well on my own quest to ditch the Panic for good, but leave it to a WMD to send my spirits crashing down. At a recent dinner party, the married host clued me in to another Doree. Is it possible, I thought to myself, that in this world there could be a duplication of wit, charm, and panic in a namesake counterpart? Who was this poseur and what was she doing hijacking my good name?

The eerie similarity didn't stop there. It seems this Dory (at least we spelled it differently) was engaged (okay, annoying enough). What's worse is that Bizarro Dory's wedding was in just three months (getting more annoying by the second) and that she was engaged to a guy she met the same day—at the same event—where I'd met my ex-PF! So there I had been, in the same room, flashing my cleavage and attention at my since-departed PF while Bizarro Dory was zeroing in on her future husband!

So at the dinner party, instead of discussing *my* wedding plans with *my* fiancé whom I'd met at the same time, I had to politely suffer in silence through a fellow guest's discourse on the government's cover-up of renewable energy sources. What's worse, Bizarro Dory and I were apparently living parallel lives—we are both svelte blondes, we both live on the same street—except for one difference: she got the life that was clearly supposed to be mine!

"He really gets me," gushed Bizarro Dory, flashing an okay ring. See, I thought, she too has been misunderstood all these years and yearns for someone to see the real her—the real person behind all the layers of beauty and brilliance. Though if her raison d'être is to get married, how complex could she be? But if I can't get married right now, neither should she! "Where's the sisterly solidarity?" I wondered. But then I realized that was something the *old* Doree would say—not this newly enlightened one! So to further my own personal growth, I'm as happy as I can be for the young couple (. . . as *I* can be, that is).

Remember, with word of every new engagement that comes your way, the Panic Years will try their hardest to grip you and keep you in their clutches for good. But you must disentangle yourself. Set yourself free, for when you emerge, ring or no ring, you will see that a free and reclaimed life feels much better against your skin than the Panic does.

Examine what it is you really want out of life, and if it still means tying the knot—and subsequent leash—around his neck, then go about it healthfully and in good measure so the Panic Years don't become the Straitjacket Years, making for a desperate(ly) unfashionable single girl combo. History hasn't put its Panic Years stamp on you yet. It's never too late to change your course by changing your attitude and moving beyond the Panic—with or without some engagement bling.

A good friend of mine recently shared some of the most poignant advice I've ever heard, and I know it will stay with me for some time. "You just have to relax," she said. "I was at the point where I acknowledged either it will happen or it won't, and if it doesn't happen that's okay too." It looks like there's something to her advice: she's happily married now, living in a classic six in one of Manhattan's toniest zip codes and regularly attends those annoying society brunches. Bitch.

It's when we're most natural—most true to ourselves— that we're at our personal best and when we will most likely find someone who gravitates to us for the depth of our character, not the depths of our desperation. The best marriages are those in which both people retain their strong, independent selves—two self-fulfilled individuals coming together instead of two marginally whole people who cling to each other in desperate need of completion. Remember, you are nothing if not self-reliant. Marriage can never complete someone who's not completed independently of it.

And remember, when it is your turn, to distinguish your-self from the phalanx of insensitive friends who exerted that sense of superiority when they got engaged, minimizing you and whatever promotion you got at work or the apartment you just bought, thereby legitimizing the ring as the sole barometer of success.

But you needn't worry about me. I was on the receiving end of a proposal this very week. It all happened so fast. I was stuck in a crosswalk on a bustling New York City street when all of a sudden I heard sustained honking accompanied by the abuse of double negatives left and right. "Hey, Beautiful!" the lovesick lothario shouted so everyone (the pretzel stand oper-ator and Amish tourists alike) could hear the admiration in his voice. "I'll marry you if you get out of my way." And just like that, it happened for me. Even Pretzel Guy said, "Go for it!"

I know the relationship's young, but it sounds promising.

When I first started exploring the phenomenon of Panic, I had no intention of making myself a career panicker. And so, I'm getting out. Maybe next year I'll even break with tra-dition and have my birthday party at a venue other than Macy's bridal salon. I'm ready to pass the panic torch on to a new generation. With any luck, I'll be married and divorced by 2016.

Acknowledgments

There are many incredible people in my life who have helped make this book possible. And to those who so wholly believe in me, I believe in you more.

Thank you to all my friends and contacts who were so giving of themselves by sharing their stories and opening their hearts, allowing me to publish their innermost thoughts and feelings. I guess I used "this doesn't leave this room" as a figure of speech. . . . Your experiences will touch the lives of readers everywhere who can benefit from your extraordinary openness.

There would be no book without the uncompromising cheering section that is my family—especially my mom. Your unfailing love, support, editorial guidance, and killer instincts have made me what I am today: a post-Panicker with one dream checked off. As constant a source of material as you might be—you're Panic by Proxy, but I love you anyway!—you have given your all to me to help ensure the success of this book. And of course, thank you to Ize, without whom there would have been no Panic Years in my life.

Paula Balzer has my deep gratitude for championing this book from the beginning, and her constant encouragement means so much. And profuse thanks to everyone at Broadway Books, including Ann Campbell, Laura Lee Mattingly, Ellen Folan, and the rest of the incredible team that helped deliver *The Panic Years* and make it the best it could be.